Also from WriteGirl Publications

Intensity: The 10th Anniversary Anthology from WriteGirl

Beyond Words: The Creative Voices of WriteGirl

Silhouette: Bold Lines & Voices from WriteGirl

Listen to Me: Shared Secrets from WriteGirl

Lines of Velocity: Words that Move from WriteGirl

Untangled: Stories & Poetry from the Women and Girls of WriteGirl

Nothing Held Back: Truth & Fiction from WriteGirl

Pieces of Me: The Voices of WriteGirl

Bold Ink: Collected Voices of Women and Girls

Threads

Pens on Fire: Creative Writing Experiments for Teens from WriteGirl (Curriculum Guide)

In-Schools Program Anthologies

No Matter What: Creative Voices from the WriteGirl In-Schools Program

So Much To Say: The Creative Voices of the WriteGirl In-Schools Program

Sound of My Voice: Bold Words from the WriteGirl In-Schools Program

This is Our Space: Bold Words from the WriteGirl In-Schools Program

Ocean of Words: Bold Voices from the WriteGirl In-Schools Program

Reflections: Creative Writing from Destiny Girls Academy

Afternoon Shine: Creative Writing from the Bold Ink Writers Program at the Marc & Eva Stern Math and Science School

Words That Echo: Creative Writing from Downey, Lawndale and Lynwood Cal-SAFE Schools

The Landscape Ahead: Creative Writing from New Village Charter High School

Sometimes, Just Sometimes: Creative Writing from La Vida West and Lynwood Cal-SAFE Programs

Everything About Her: Creative Writing from New Village High School

Visible Voices: Creative Writing from Destiny Girls Academy

Now That I Think About It: Creative Writing from Destiny Girls Academy

Look at Me Long Enough: Creative Writing from Destiny Girls Academy

Acclaim for WriteGirl Publications

Praise for *No Character Limit: Truth & Fiction from WriteGirl*

"WriteGirl is an important force in a world where sometimes words are the only thing we have to save us."
— **Francesca Lia Block, author, the *Weetzie Bat book series*, *House of Dolls*, *The Elementals***

"The writings in *No Character Limit* are bold and passionate. The words grab you, shake you and invade your brain but most of all they make you grateful – grateful that these girls are writing, sharing with us their unique perspectives on the human condition."
— **Jennifer Crittenden, television writer/producer, *The New Adventures of Old Christine*, *Arrested Development*, *Everybody Loves Raymond***

"This collection is staggering. WriteGirl is a phenomenal incubator for greatness and allows girls to not only find their voice, but to celebrate it."
— **Heather Hach, screenwriter, *What to Expect When You're Expecting*, *Legally Blonde: The Musical*, *Freaky Friday***

Praise for *Intensity: The 10th Anniversary Anthology from WriteGirl*

"Many writers think, 'I can't,' or 'I'm not good at this,' or 'I don't know how to spell the words.' But the best way a writer can overcome self-doubt is to keep writing. These girls started with a few words and the seed of an idea. With WriteGirl's encouragement, each girl allowed the words to keep coming until her idea grew into an essay, a story, or a poem. What do writers do? They write. And how lucky we are to have these writers' words and ideas to inspire us!"
— **Carole King, GRAMMY Award-winning singer and songwriter**

"Girls passionate about writing is what carries this book. A compilation of mentor and mentee compositions, the anthology is a beautiful tour of teen views on everything from nature and family to food and color. The book also contains "Writing Experiments," providing inspiring examples on a specific topic and challenging the reader to become the writer. The editors have discovered budding talent in many young women. This is a great anniversary edition and will inspire other teens with its creativity and passion."
— **Eric Hoffer Award Committee, Honorable Mention, Young Adult Category**

"The work of these young women reminds me what it's like to be young. Their voices are clear and passionate, carefully observant and exuberant. They celebrate their friends, their neighborhoods, new love, and mourn the losses from which their youth can't shield them. They tell the truth."
— **Terry Wolverton, author, *Insurgent Muse: Life and Art at the Woman's Building***

Praise for *Beyond Words: The Creative Voices of WriteGirl*

"There is nothing more powerful than thoughts and nothing more damaging than having no outlet for expressing those thoughts. *Beyond Words* is that outlet. For these young women, this anthology represents mental and emotion liberation via pens, pencils, and keyboard strokes."
— **Felicia D. Henderson, television writer/Executive Producer, *Fringe*, *Gossip Girl***

"Powerful and strong, raw and vulnerable – these are the voices of girls who demand to be heard. Girls who know their words have real meaning, in a world that can often feel anything but real. WriteGirl's latest anthology, *Beyond Words*, is proof of their conviction. You will not only hear them, but you'll never forget them."

– **Kami Garcia, New York Times Bestselling Author of** *Beautiful Creatures*

"Writing is the level playing field. No matter how rich or poor, tall or short, pretty or plain, if you can write, you can find personal fulfillment, build self-confidence and influence others to help your dreams become realities. Kudos to WriteGirl for providing young, female writers in our city the chance to learn the art of communication. The power of your program is evident on each and every page of your latest anthology, *Beyond Words*."

– **Lynda Resnick, entrepreneur, author,** *Rubies in the Orchard*

"Write what you know, write with passion. You won't find a greater group to offer that up than teen girls! If you want inspiring, gutsy, heartfelt stories, and you don't have access to a diary – here are voices, strong and passionate. Having been a part of a WriteGirl workshop – all I could think was, "Why didn't I have this support when I was a teen?!" We all want to be heard. I love what these girls have done with this book."

– **Rita Hsiao, screenwriter,** *Toy Story 2, Mulan*

"Writing has been my life and I work very hard at it. Having a group like WriteGirl is an amazing help to those who love the craft. The mentoring of the young girls is a wonderful way to pair the professional with the new writers to show them how to hone their skills and have a successful career doing so. The excerpts written by these girls are inspiring and show genuine talent. I give a big thumbs up to WriteGirl and to those who are working hard to do what they love so much."

– **Diane Warren, Grammy Award-winning songwriter, "Because You Loved Me"**

"WriteGirl is a life changing program that reaches out and supports young women to express themselves through writing. The dedicated mentors who do the hard work with them are guardian angels. And I suspect it is as life changing for them as it is for the young authors."

– **Naomi Foner, screenwriter,** *Bee Season, Losing Isaiah, Running On Empty*

"Cheers to Keren Taylor for coming up with the dream of giving teenage girls a voice, and then creating an organization that made her dream a reality. Cheers also for her hardworking staff, and the dedicated volunteers and mentors of WriteGirl for enabling teenage girls to wrestle the truth of their lives, their hearts and souls, into literary form on the page. And another round of cheers for *Beyond Words*, the latest addition to WriteGirl's growing library of award winning anthologies."

– **Barbara Abercrombie, writer, UCLA Extension Creative Writing Instructor,**
Cherished: 21 Writers on Animals They've Loved and Lost (Editor)

"*Beyond Words* is an anthology alive with discovery, humor, and a keen examination of the world through the written word…It is truly delicious paging through this anthology, stumbling on lines such as these and those by 17-year-old Mikayla Cowley, "You know you're done with this world / When you're swimming into walls." This is exactly what WriteGirl is all about: removing walls so that girls like Mikayla can swim out to sea."

– **Sholeh Wolpe, poet,** *Rooftops of Tehran*

"The WriteGirls are woman warriors of the pen. To read their poems and stories is to be heartened by their wonderful, inspiring, regenerating powers."

– **Maxine Hong Kingston, author,** *The Woman Warrior, The Fifth Book of Peace,*
I Love a Broad Margin to My Life

Praise for *Silhouette: Bold Lines & Voices from WriteGirl*

"WriteGirl is essential to helping our young women know how important their thoughts and feelings, not just their looks and bodies, are. Right on, girls – WriteGirl!"

– **Nikki Giovanni, poet,** *Bicycles: Love Poems, Blues: For All the Changes,*
Quilting the Black-Eyed Pea

"WriteGirl is one of the most inspirational, innovative, charming projects gracing the contemporary literary scene. And *Silhouette* is one of its finer manifestations. These girls really *CAN* write!"

– **Carolyn See, author,** *There Will Never Be Another You, Making a Literary Life*

"*Silhouette* is inspiring and WriteGirl is a great model for writers and teachers who are looking for ways to improve literacy and to help teens become successful through writing."

– **Elfrieda Abbe, Publisher,** *The Writer Magazine*

"So many know the woes of the writer. The struggle, the scraping by, the rejection. But beyond the mass of cigarette smoke and rejection letters exists a new start to a writing career. A clean one. A mentored one. An uplifting one. It's called WriteGirl…Until girls from around the country can access the beauty in one-on-one mentoring and a varied writing education, each anthology from WriteGirl offers a small taste of the experience."

– *ForeWord Magazine* **Review**

"These are breathtaking works that explode with emotional daring, formal elegance and searing honesty. WriteGirl has unleashed a host of exciting new writing voices into our midst. Readers everywhere: take note!"

– **Marisa Silver, author,** *Alone With You, Babe in Paradise, The God of War*

Praise for *Listen to Me: Shared Secrets from WriteGirl*

"The wit and wisdom found inside *Listen to Me* comes in whispers, shouts, giggles, cries, chortles, inner ahas, and other creative noises – proving once again that the voices of women and girls are as rich and varied as a great symphony. WriteGirl's newest anthology hits your funny bone in new places, strums your heart strings and strikes just the right chords to make your imagination sing. Listen to me, do yourself a favor and pay attention to what's being said in *Listen to Me*."

– **Jane Wagner, writer/producer/director,** *The Incredible Shrinking Woman,*
The Search for Signs of Intelligent Life in the Universe

"I love hearing the new voices in these pages. I've had the pleasure of being part of one of WriteGirl's workshops…Now when I meet a young woman in her teens who asks for advice on becoming a writer, I instantly say, "Have you heard of WriteGirl? Get involved with them immediately!"

– **Robin Swicord, screenwriter and director,** *The Curious Case of Benjamin Button,*
The Jane Austen Book Club, Memoirs of a Geisha

"WriteGirl is a dazzling chorus of smart, tough, inspired voices of independent-minded young women. Their mentors are professional writers who understand how important it is to let these voices be heard… WriteGirl is opening up a whole new connection to the imaginations of young women – and I say Brava!"

> – Carol Muske-Dukes, poet, novelist and California Poet Laureate, *Channeling Mark Twain, Sparrow, Life After Death*

"*Listen to Me* is blood on paper, souls on the page. What courage these young writers have, what generosity. Once again, the girls and women of WriteGirl challenge us all to step into our voices with confidence and grace, and to sing."

> – Sarah Fain, Co-Executive Producer/writer, *Dollhouse, The Shield, Lie To Me*

Praise for *Lines of Velocity: Words That Move from WriteGirl*

"Unlike many such anthologies, this collection *[Lines of Velocity]* includes the work of experienced mentors…as well as the teen participants. The result is a dynamic exchange of shared prompts, ideas, and projects…The writing is at times hilarious…At other times, it is heartbreaking…This anthology is sure to be picked up by aspiring young writers as well as educators looking for inspired samples and interactive exercises."

> – *School Library Journal*

"*Lines of Velocity* is full of magic: Not just the wonder of raw, vivid writing; but also the alchemy of writers, leaping across age and cultural divides to inspire each other. The resulting work crackles with energy."

> – Carol Flint, television writer/producer, *ER, The West Wing*

"*Lines of Velocity* sparks with the lively intelligence of gifted young writers well on their way to discovering the power of language. If I'd had the WriteGirl experience at the onset of my formative years, who knows? I might be a Pulitzer Prize winner by now."

> – Suzanne Lummis, poet and teacher, *In Danger (The California Poetry Series)*

Praise for *Untangled: Stories & Poetry from the Women and Girls of WriteGirl*

"This fifth anthology…is a worthwhile and highly motivational compendium of poetry, short stories, nonfiction and dramatic excerpts from both students and teachers. Including great topic suggestions, writing experiments and insight into the creative process, this volume is a perfect fit for the high school classroom. Sharp observations abound…unconventional writing exercises… motivational quotes…nonstop inspiration."

> – *Publishers Weekly*

"*Untangled* gives me hope, riles me up, revs me up, makes me sad, makes me happy, makes me want to write, and makes me want to read. All I ever think about is how to make more young women want to share their voices with the world – and WriteGirl, plus this anthology – are actually doing it. There's nothing cooler than jumping into the worlds of these young women as well as the minds of the brilliant women who mentor them. *Untangled* rocks!"

> – Jill Soloway, writer/producer, *United States of Tara*; author of *Tiny Ladies in Shiny Pants*

"This is the kind of book that makes you want to get up and shout about the power of writing and the power of women. It's impossible to ignore these teen writers, the pen-holders of a new generation of words, and their talented mentors."

    – Christina Kim, television writer, *Miami Medical, Ghost Whisperer, Lost*

"The writing here, always moving and sometimes painful, displays freshness, an exuberant inventiveness, and – surprisingly – a hard-won wisdom. Some of these young women will undoubtedly grow up to be poets, journalists and novelists. All of them have already learned to write honestly and with conviction."

    – Benjamin Schwarz, literary and national editor, *The Atlantic*

Praise for *Nothing Held Back: Truth & Fiction from WriteGirl*

"For these girls (and their mentors) writing is a lens, a filter, a way to cut through the nonsense and see the possibilities...[Nothing Held Back] suggests that reports of literacy's death have been greatly exaggerated, that language remains a transformative force."

    – David Ulin, Editor, *Los Angeles Times Book Review*

Praise for *Pieces of Me: The Voices of WriteGirl*

"Wow! I couldn't stop reading this. Talk about goosebumps! This book will shock you – and make you think – and make you *FEEL* – all at the same time!"

    – R.L. Stine, author, *Goosebumps* and *Fear Street series*

"All the boldness, unselfconsciousness, lack of vanity and beautiful raw talent that is usually tamped down by adulthood bursts from these pages and announces a formidable new crop of young writers."

    – Meghan Daum, author, *Life Would Be Beautiful If I Lived In That House* and *My Misspent Youth*

"*Pieces of Me* is a riveting collection of creative writing produced by girls and women with enormous talent. On every page you'll encounter fresh voices and vibrant poems and stories that pull you into these writers' worlds, into the energy of their lives."

    – Vendela Vida, author, *Away We Go, Let the Northern Lights Erase Your Name*

Awards for WriteGirl Publications

2012   **Honorable Mention**, Eric Hoffer Award, Young Adult: Intensity
2012   **Winner**, International Book Awards, Anthologies: Non-Fiction: Intensity
2012   **Winner**, National Indie Excellence Awards, Anthologies: Intensity
2012   **Runner-Up**, San Francisco Book Festival Awards, Anthologies: Intensity
2012   **Runner-Up**, Paris Book Festival Awards, Anthologies: Intensity
2011   **Finalist**, ForeWord Reviews Book of the Year Awards, Anthologies: Intensity
2011   **Honorable Mention**, Los Angeles Book Festival, Anthologies: Intensity
2011   **Winner**, London Book Festival Awards, Anthologies: Intensity
2011   **Honorable Mention**, New England Book Festival, Anthologies: Intensity
2011   **Finalist**, USA Best Book Awards, Anthologies, Nonfiction: Intensity
2011   **Winner**, International Book Awards, Anthologies, Non-Fiction: Beyond Words
2011   **Winner**, National Indie Excellence Awards, Anthologies: Beyond Words
2011   **Finalist**, Next Generation Indie Book Awards, Anthologies: Beyond Words
2011   **Finalist**, Independent Book Publisher Awards, Anthologies: Beyond Words
2010   **Finalist**, ForeWord Reviews Book of the Year Awards, Anthologies, Beyond Words
2010   **Winner**, London Book Festival, Anthologies: Beyond Words
2010   **Winner**, National Best Book Awards, USA BookNews, Poetry: Beyond Words
2010   **First Place**, Anthologies, National Indie Excellence Awards: Silhouette
2010   **Winner**, New York Book Festival, Teenage: Silhouette
2010   **Winner**, International Book Awards, Anthologies: Silhouette
2010   **First Place**, Anthologies, National Indie Excellence Awards: Silhouette
2009   **Winner**, London Book Festival Awards, Anthologies: Silhouette
2009   **Finalist**, ForeWord Reviews Book of the Year Awards: Silhouette
2009   **Winner**, Los Angeles Book Festival, Nonfiction: Silhouette
2009   **Winner**, National Best Book Awards, USA Book News, Anthologies: Silhouette
2009   **Silver Medal**, Independent Publisher Book Awards: Listen to Me
2009   **Runner-Up**, San Francisco Book Festival, Teenage: Listen to Me
2009   **Winner**, National Indie Excellence Awards, Anthologies: Listen to Me
2009   **Runner Up**, New York Book Festival, Teenage: Listen to Me
2009   **Finalist**, Next Generation Indie Book Awards: Listen to Me
2008   **Finalist**, ForeWord Reviews: Listen to Me
2008   **Winner**, London Book Festival Awards, Teenage: Lines of Velocity
2008   **Honorable Mention**, New England Books Festival, Anthologies: Lines of Velocity
2008   **Grand Prize Winner**, Next Generation Indie Book Awards: Lines of Velocity
2008   **Winner**, National Best Book Awards, USA Book News: Lines of Velocity
2008   **Silver Medal**, Independent Publisher Awards: Lines of Velocity
2008   **Honorable Mention**, New York Festival of Books Awards: Lines of Velocity
2007   **Finalist**, ForeWord Magazine: Lines of Velocity
2007   **Honorable Mention**, London Book Festival Awards: Untangled
2006   **Finalist**, ForeWord Magazine: Untangled
2006   **Winner**, National Best Book Awards, USA Book News: Untangled
2006   **Notable Mention**, Writers Notes Magazine Book Awards: Nothing Held Back
2005   **Finalist**, Independent Publisher Awards: Pieces of Me
2005   **Finalist**, ForeWord Magazine: Bold Ink

No
Character
Limit

Truth & Fiction from WriteGirl

www.writegirl.org

A WriteGirl Publication

WriteGirl Publications
Los Angeles

No Character Limit: Truth & Fiction from WriteGirl

Publisher & Editor: Keren Taylor

Associate Editors: Abby Anderson

Cindy Collins

Jia-Rui Cook

Allison Deegan

Rachel Fain

Kirsten Giles

Rachel Hogue

Brande Jackson

Rachel Kaminer

Diahann Reyes

Art Director: Keren Taylor

Book Design: Velvette De Laney

Printing: Chromatic Inc., Los Angeles

FIRST EDITION
Printed in the United States of America

Orders, inquiries and correspondence:
WriteGirl Publications
Los Angeles, California
www.writegirl.org
213-253-2655

Acknowledgements

Many individuals and organizations contributed to creating the lively community reflected in this book. We thank all of you.

Thank you to every WriteGirl member for making this book possible. Each spring, the WriteGirl book production team dives into an intensive four-month project of producing a new anthology. Book submissions arrive in all forms: Some follow every guideline, from meeting the deadline in perfectly typed 12-point Arial font, to handwritten, hastily faxed notebook pages that take an entire de-coding team to decipher. Some of the work was inspired in a Los Angeles minute at a WriteGirl workshop; other pieces were crafted over months of mentor-mentee meetings at a coffee shop. Some are short bursts of inspiration; others are excerpts from novels and screenplays in progress. In every submission, we see a unique point-of-view and that intriguing variety sets the direction for the book.

Thank you to all our WriteGirl parents. Our events this year were held throughout the greater Los Angeles area, and we appreciate your enthusiasm in ensuring your girl's participation. You are a vital driving force, literally and metaphorically.

Thank you WriteGirl volunteers for your commitment and dedication. You create the supportive environment that allows girls to share their perspectives freely and develop their voices. We thank you for generously sharing your time and expertise.

To our growing network of supporters and friends, thank you for helping sustain WriteGirl and making it possible for us to expand our programming and partnerships.

Thank you for the Herculean efforts of everyone who made it possible for each graduating senior to leave for college with her own copy of this book, hot off the presses.

Finally, thank you to all of our teen writers. Your willingness to express yourselves in a variety of genres, to sit down and write when you didn't feel like it, to make time for workshops and regular meetings with your mentor while juggling a host of activities and pressures in your teen lives, to read your work to audiences small and large inspires us all. Your energy and creativity are contagious. Your bold and clear voices are limitless.

Table of Contents

Write from your heart
and not your mind.
Fall into the arms
of writing.

Foreword

When I was in the sixth grade, my grandmother gave me a diary for Christmas. It was the fancy kind that came with a lock and key. I should have been thrilled, but for weeks I was too scared to write in it. What did I have to say that was important enough to be written into a book? And wasn't it wrong to keep secrets from your family, even your nosey little brothers?

When my mother heard why I wasn't using the diary, she said:

"Sometimes writing about your problems can help you figure out ways to work through them… *especially* ones about your nosey little brothers. Go on, girl. Write!"

After that, I began writing in my diary all the time. I had a *lot* of problems to work through.

Soon I began to suspect that my nosey little brothers had figured out a way to break into my diary and read it when I wasn't looking. That's when I got an idea. I started keeping my *real* diary in a notebook marked *Algebra*, and writing fake entries in the fancy diary about how the actual Meg Cabot had been kidnapped by aliens. The Meg Cabot who lived in our house was a clone who'd been left in her place.

One day I came home to find my two little brothers crying, clinging to my mother's legs in terror as they stared up at me. My mother was holding my fancy diary, open to the latest entry. She looked annoyed.

"Meggin Patricia Cabot," she said. "Tell your brothers that you are not a clone from outer space."

I apologized. I should have been upset that *I* was the one who was in trouble for lying, not my brothers for invading my privacy. But I wasn't. It was one of the best days of my life. No number one slot on the bestseller list, not even seeing my own name on a movie screen, with "based on the book by" in front of it, has ever come close.

Because that was the day I realized that words have power, and that through them, *we* have power, too…the power to make someone laugh, the power to make someone cry, but most of all, *the power to make someone believe.*

That's what WriteGirl is all about: Giving girls power through words. Not only the power to solve their own problems, but the power to make other people believe, and truly hear what girls have to say.

In this book, what these girls have to say makes us laugh at times, and other times, makes us want to cry. But their words always make us believe. These girls understand the power of words. I believe these girls will go on to use that power wisely and well for years to come.

Go on, girl. Write!

> – Meg Cabot
> Author, *The Princess Diaries, Allie Finkle's Rules for Girls, Size 12* and *Ready to Rock*

Introduction

WriteGirl is about building character, gradually, over time, the way anything precious and wonderful develops. The WriteGirl season is nine months long, giving girls and women time to get to know each other, try writing in new genres, share their creative work with each other and eventually perform for large audiences, such as at the Writers Guild of America Theater. As much as WriteGirl is about helping girls develop their creative voices, it is also about building their confidence, their resilience and their courage.

If you stepped into the room at one of our monthly creative writing workshops, the intense focus of the women writers is as palpable as the cautious openness of the teen girls beside them. It is clear that there is a lot more happening in the room than just writing and it never fails to move me deeply.

This year, we have welcomed new partnerships with some of the most prestigious civic institutions in Los Angeles. We brought our annual Songwriting Workshop to the GRAMMY Museum, our Journalism Workshop to the Los Angeles Times headquarters, and our Character & Dialogue Workshop to the Museum of Contemporary Art, just to name a few. We are very grateful for support from these outstanding partners. The added inspiration of being surrounded by great art, artists and writers, made our workshops even more electric than usual. The writers' muse seemed to hover a little closer – so much so that we have an entire chapter in this book dedicated to her and all her permutations.

This book showcases our creativity, but also our community. As we conclude year eleven, thousands of women and girls, and many supporters, have contributed to the WriteGirl movement, and to all of our collective and individual achievements. *No Character Limit* demonstrates the best of how our community creates, feels and lives.

As with all WriteGirl anthologies, there are personal writing tips from our members throughout the book and a full chapter of creative writing experiments to inspire limitless stories and characters. So set caution aside, and enter here!

> – Keren Taylor
> Founder and Executive Director, WriteGirl

1 *Identity*

On a Quest

WRITE WHEN YOUR EMOTION IS OVERFLOWING. EXPERIENCE MAKES ALL THE DIFFERENCE.

Katherine Bolton-Ford, age 17

During a weekly session with my mentor, we each wrote a piece using the words "admit, spiritual, special, grate," and "whirl." I liked the rhythm that came to me while writing this poem and the strength it gave me at the end.

Spiritual Nothings

I'll admit that I've forgotten
What it's like in your arms
To come home to a place with four walls
I'll confess that I walk
The line of spiritual nothings
The world, as it turns,
Passing me by
I'll reveal myself
As if it's nothing special
Through words and lines
You won't understand
My truth, it hurts
Grates just beneath the surface
Begging you to find me, if you can
My secrets, they whisper
Dust in the sunlight
Twirling as the sand
My footsteps, they leave me
Taking something with them
Something I never knew
I'll accept that I'll forget
What it is you've taught me
But I've just met my confidence
I'll never let her leave me
And I'll never let you hurt me again

Diahann Reyes, mentor

We moved all the time growing up. I wrote this when my parents moved out of the last house where my sister and I had lived with them.

Dry Oak Drive

10 years of a lifetime, 10 years of 4 lives spent.
A place to reconnect. A stopover between all worlds.
A place of refuge. Reunion. A place to hide. To reinvent.

A place to nurture a broken heart. Rebuild relationships.
Find ourselves. Redefine ourselves.

A place to grow rich. Plant the seeds from which to sprout
a new kind of life. To store our memories that are too
heavy to lug around, yet too precious not to keep.

A place for hellos and goodbyes, 'til the goodbyes become hellos
And there is no longer any separation between the two.
Thanks to Skype, text messaging, Facebook, and North by
Southwest Air.

A place to grow new roots. Be a child again.
The world kept away outside wooden doors and sliding gate
Where all that exists is family.
And mommy and daddy to mind the locks, cook the food,
walk the perimeter and basically take care of everything.

And all I have to do is stay in bed all day,
Because I know I am safe and their world revolves around me.

Rachael Morris, age 16

Trespasser

Letters construct a word
Like a hologram of colored images
Through even the deepest darkest dwellings of my brain
Using photonics to guide them on the walls of my skull
Words dictate writing
Creating imagery in my head
Words create worlds
I cannot call my own
I am a lowly trespasser into the worlds
Words weave

Yujane Chen, age 14

I've never exactly been a look-you-in-the-eye type of person, so when I'm looking down, I see shoes. That got me thinking about other people and the lives they live and walk through each day...well, you know the rest.

Shoes

I still remember when I was barefoot, young,
nothing to worry about weighing me down
But now the sand has lines drawn like barbed wire to walk on
I'm searching for a pair of shoes
Shoes that don't fit exactly, take time to grow into
I don't know what they'll look like
Maybe like navy blue mary janes from second grade
Maybe plain old sneakers – you know, the kind for burning rubber
Maybe those old oxfords a man wears because he can't buy new ones
Maybe like that
Or maybe like lotus shoes, forever painfully binding beauty
Red shiny galoshes that splash and scatter puddles to raindrop dreams
Flip-flops or sling-backs for lazy summers
Maybe like Dorothy's, taking me home,
Or Cinderella's, promising Happily Ever After
I wish for shoes to walk around in, like a white-collar lawyer marching,
Or sprinting in Nikes like an Olympic athlete getting gold every
single time
Or sauntering in street shoes that say I'm-just-like-everyone-else-
not-any-different
Maybe like that

I'm wishing I had them
They must be somewhere, maybe I'm not looking hard enough
When I find them, I'll let you know

Carly Pandza, mentor

After eating very spicy Asian food for dinner, my mouth was on fire and I thought, "What a great line!"

My Mouth Is on Fire

My mouth is on fire with words unspoken.
If I fail to let these flames burn, will they die completely
to no more than faded embers in a fireplace or fire pit on the beach?
Remnants of opinions and philosophies that could change the world,
but instead they raged, then flickered, then died.

All because of the fear to release the fire,
afraid that someone else can't stand the heat
of the truth, of that voice that speaks to us every day,
every moment,
but we silence it with logic and cruelty to keep it in its place.

I want to free that voice,
that fire that burns from a place far deeper than my mouth
until the flames are raging so fiercely that no one
can escape the heat of it,
until every lie, building, tree and car is engorged
in its fury and all that is left is a world that is on fire
and everyone standing around
wondering how they are going to put it out.

Nicole Nitta, age 17

I associate myself with the nighttime. After a sleepless night, I heard the sound of an owl outside my window just as the sun was rising.

Night's Allure

Amidst a midnight daydream, I was snapped back to reality
by the whistle of a lonely morning train
that echoed through my thin apartment walls.
I wonder if it felt as disconnected from its journey
as I felt for my own life at such an ungodly hour.
At times, light from the house next door would shine through my blinds
coaxing out hidden shadows around me.

Summer days in Los Angeles are cruel and unforgiving
as are the nights.
But this summer was different.
Each day, the sun stretched out its rays just enough to keep the
city warm.
Night was cool and crisp, like a glass of iced tea.
The air was intoxicating, pleasing and easy on all the senses.
With each breath, it became easier to forget
all the worries that existed in daylight.

I never knew my neighborhood had owls until I became one myself
I was separated from the day walkers,
overlooking the world as it rested peacefully.

As the moon slips away in a luxurious amethyst sea,
clouds are set ablaze in shades of morning tangerine.

Today is another day,
another day I'll sleep away.
Goodnight sun.

get up and get over being shy - shake all that anxiety and write.

Marni Rader, mentor

This was inspired by all of our incredible WriteGirls. It celebrates determination, and believing in yourself no matter what anyone else tells you.

Anthem

Who says I can't be great?
Pirouette on the edges of others' expectations, then leap,
arcing so wide and far that I no longer see them.
Who says I can't sparkle, bursting with a brilliance
so bright and sharp that it shocks?

More than you think I can.
More than he wants me to.
More than they thought I would ever have the nerve to do.

I may writhe under thickening layers of jealousy, fear, even love and
protection,
from friends and family suffocating me,
Trying to keep all of us safe by keeping me small.
But I will breathe.
Like curling, fragile, green tendrils breaking through concrete,
with a heartbeat that begs to grow.

Yes, it's my choice.
Yes, I'm talking to those of you who never knew me 'cuz you never tried.
Who says I can't uncurl against the 10,000 pounds of pressure
that is what everybody else thinks?
Free the already living, growing greatness that is I.

Who says I can't...you?
Watch me.

Donna Ramirez, age 14

The Eyes

The eyes
see everything,
record everything that was
wonderful,
drop tears
to erase
something
that was hurtful.

Monice Mitchell Simms, mentor

I wrote this poem after a particularly difficult day of mentoring at the Road to Success Academy.

Adolescent Hearts

She's soft inside.
A warm gooey mess,
heart not safety-pinned to her sleeve.

It beats outside her chest,
to compensate.
She distracts you.
She downright attacks you.
Enraged,

while the others,
their wounded adolescent hearts protruding,
bear witness.

Jenny Gonzalez, age 18

Wonderful

I am a sunflower,
now and forever devoted
to the skies, the sun and rain.

The rain pelts me with its tears,
and when plucked,
I am so angry, I cry sunflower seeds.
And when the great ball of Apollo's fire
shines on me,
filling me with power and energy,
I blossom.

Smiling at happy blue skies.
Standing bright as the sunrise.

Screaming at the skies,
and the sun and rain.

Berna Roberts, mentor

I have three sisters and four nieces, so I often find myself reflecting on the different places I was in my life at those ages.

Excerpt from "Becoming"

I was tired of being someone else
So I went inside myself and dusted off my innards
Polished my soul
Caressed my heart and held my hand over the hole it came with
at birth
Everything gleamed with shine
Brand new and fresh
I looked at myself and I saw me
What I was and what I'd been hiding my whole life

I spoke to myself, barely recognizing my own voice
I told myself, "I love you. It's not your fault. I forgive you. You
are beautiful."
A tension, a weight
The heavy burden of self-loathing, self-hate and regrets
Lifted
Rose from my body
A darkness shot out of my fingertips, my toes, my ears, my nose
A guttural sound escaped my mouth to release the pain of self-denial
And in that moment
I could feel, I knew
I was becoming a beautiful woman.

While ~~either~~ you're writing, pretend it's all perfect.

Melanie Ballesteros, age 16

I read this to Linda Albertano at the Poetry Workshop. She liked it and asked me to read it again. She told me that this poem was the opposite of what is being taught to us by society. After that, I really wanted to share this poem, so here it is.

Damsel in Modern Times

Stuck in a tower.

So overrated,
waiting for a knight to kill the dragon
and save me.
Letting witches poison me with apples,
but I have a brain.
I'm not Snow White.

We are all princesses,
we have a purpose.
Being worthy,
knowing what to do.
It's inside of us, since…forever.

We look for love
in gold, glory, and men,
but it's inside of us.
We don't need to be saved
by fairy tales.

By the Word of the King,
I am a Princess,
even after THE END.

Bianca Primavera, age 13

This poem is dedicated to a friend of mine who hides all of her feelings inside, not talking to anyone about her problems.

Smile

Everyone has different smiles,
but yours is one of a kind.

Behind your smile lies a deep frown.
Sorrow, pain, guilt and anger
build up inside your heart.

You hide it from everybody else
but maybe it's time
to open up,
to know that you're not alone in this world.

I'm always here,
whenever you feel discouraged.

I'm always here,
to make your day brighter than yellow.
I'm always here to hear you out.

Tell me your problems, your pain, your sorrow.
Count on me whenever you feel discouraged.

I'm always here to cheer you on
and make your day brighter than yellow.

2 Nature

Track a
Comet

Aunye Scott-Anderson, age 16

Nature Feels

There are mint leaves crushed
beneath my shoulder blades,
sage tangled in my hair,
lemon zest hangs down
like silk strands from broken spiderwebs.
My voice echoes in the trunk of the ugly fruit tree,
its plump and bulbous fruit,
bumpy and enormous.

Here in the garden, I plant my soul
beside the rose bushes, the thorns as my protection,
my hummingbirds visit The Rose of Charon,
the greying dead branches, thin and decrepit,
still produce their purple and white blossoms
like a child opening its eyes.

Join me, where my sprouting surrealism
is as brilliant as marigolds.
I will share the poems inscribed on the insides of my skull
as you rest,
drinking the nectar of innocent immortality.
You and me, lying in salty moist soil,
is exactly how nature feels.

Your vulnerability, sensitivity, and most puzzling uncomfortable emotions are your greatest sources of artistic strength.

Calia Anderson, age 17

In my Art History class, we learned about Arcadia, a mythological place where man lives in harmony with nature. On a recent trip to Arkansas, I was surprised to see how many trees and wild animals there were in comparison to Los Angeles. This piece is a reflection on my relationship with nature and the idea of an Arcadian lifestyle.

Arcadia

I am not supposed to be here. The trees whisper warnings as I approach them – I don't listen. I slip off my new shoes out of respect, then step into the dense forest. I wiggle my toes in the soft dirt, thinking of the rough concrete at home. My heart swells as I look up at the army of trees surrounding me. I have stumbled upon a place that surpasses my roughly-sketched visions of paradise and mythical gardens untouched by man.

Two birds chase each other through the tree trunks, snapping playfully as their small bodies expertly dodge the surrounding branches. I look away, feeling guilty for intruding, desecrating their secret ritual with my presence. I do not fit in.

Everything about me is unnatural – my limbs are heavy, plated with cold steel. My head is a computer, creating illogical solutions to problems it can't comprehend. My heart, a broken engine, spews spirals of black smoke into the soft green leaves overhead as it tries to compensate for my lack of flesh. I leave a slick trail of oil behind me as I walk deeper into the wilderness. With each step, I grow stiffer, until I am unable to go further into this sacred space. I stand as still as a mountain and look into the sun. I pray that my parts rust over and fall off, freeing me so I can walk among the trees.

Trina Gaynon, mentor

During the Poetry Workshop, a video of a Tanya Davis poem talked about places to experience when alone. It reminded me of Prophet Rock, a writing workshop I attended a number of years ago, outside of Santa Fe.

Writers' Retreat, Monastery Library

Before even the monks rise,
I track a comet across the sky,
above the crisp snow,
bare oak trees, and Chimney Rock.

Cradling a cup of herbal tea,
I listen to the steam radiator
sing away the ice on my nose,
the numbness in my fingers.

I can hear myself breathing
as I finger a collection
of dried wildflowers to learn
the names of desert flora.

Curled up on a corner
of a deep, leather couch,
only I inhabit the book-filled room
and watch for the blush of sunrise.

Ashaki M. Jackson, mentor

I wrote this poem in honor of those who were lost in the recent tsunami off the coast of Japan.

Dissent

Our bodies give

into the ocean rolling

           us beneath its tongues How do we sing

our loss with water

brimming our throats? Oh

Sea, You

are greedy and transform us –

           our faces soft and opening in unnatural ways

You do not wash

but strike and shove as a poor parent

You rinse babies

from our arms leave husbands

waiting All

the while we spin in your disregard

your seaweeds your red so red

we confuse it with love You

upend this Body We

do not praise your reeling beauty and have nothing

to give one

who ruins consumes We

will remind you of your ways

           our monuments always whirling

in your open throat

Car'ynn Sims, age 14

that thing you walk on every day

wet, from the running sprinklers
warm, from the beaming sun
dirty, from the soil it was beside
bright, with a tone of green

I smell the earth
the raining days and the sunny
the freezing and the chilly
the first step across it to the last
the beaming future and the past
the good days and the bad
I see everything
in something so usual
as grass.

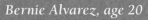

Bernie Alvarez, age 20

Summer Heat

Sandy beach, hot sun,
Ocean washes sun block off
My skin, burning for relief;
But my mind set.
Spit to the shore by waves,
Ocean grabs me.
My body can no longer swim,
I sit on the sand
As the breeze pulls me back in.

Keren Taylor, mentor

Mockingbird

I'm awakened in the middle of the night by the piercing, jagged birdcalls of the Northern Mockingbird, echoing between the buildings. The songs, while never gentle or particularly lyrical, are riveting in their range and intensity – from extremely high-pitched whines, to coarse, almost buzzer-like jabs. I even recorded a 4-minute segment on my iPhone. The screen is black when I play it back, since it was the middle of the night, but the sounds are all there – continuous and unpredictable.

It's got to wear on your self-esteem that all you do is borrow. You just listen and repeat, never offering anything original, anything uniquely your own.

Sometimes there are two birds – dueling mimics, ripping through song segments like manic magicians flipping through card tricks on a dark stage, one trying to out-do the other. At times I can tell exactly what bird they are imitating, but often they copy the neighborhood car alarms – shrieking with a borrowed and unnecessary urgency.

How do you do that? How do you keep going, with such energy, for so long?

I like the two-toned, off-balance minuet the best. It's a high warble, with two distinct notes jangling together at the same time, like young dancers stepping on the same beat, awkwardly and adorably stepping on each other.

Wikipedia says that mockingbirds, without a song of their own, typically riff through seven short cycles of a call before moving on to the next one, but whenever I try to count, I get a different number – 4 - 8 - 8 - 5 - 6 - 4. Sometimes my counting is interrupted by the blaring honk of a peacock, deep and plaintive.

Am I the only one listening? Are you also somewhere out there – sleepless, waiting and counting?

JUST PICK UP THE PEN AND
START MOVING IT OVER THE PAGE
AND DON'T STOP UNTIL THE
DOUBT GOES AWAY.

Ciara Blackwell, age 17

If you're really quiet, you can hear everything that is going on around you. The best things are heard in silence.

Heard in Silence

Huddled-up ladies walk by
pulling up at their coat collars
Leaves float by
skipping in the wind's silence
Squirrels run up trees
hiding acorns
Grass shivers
in the wind's silence
Whispers of ol' neighborhood gossip
in the wind's silence
Leaves float on by
in the wind's silence
Squirrels run by
in the wind's silence
The wind breathes a beautiful
goodnight

3 *Growing Up*

My Last SeaShore Summer

Sara Kimura, age 17

This past year has been full of changes, including a move to a different school. It's been a lot harder to stay close with one of my oldest friends. This poem reflects my feelings about our distanced relationship.

You. Me.

I wonder how long what we had
can bridge the continent between us.
It can't be long now before our memories
get sidetracked somewhere among the bustling marketplaces of
Istanbul,
and can't find their way back home again.
I'm beginning to think,
perhaps, I was mistaken.
Was there ever a we?
Or was there ever only a you,
and then a very distinctly separate, and sole,
me.
I wonder how strongly elementary school bonds are formed?
I'd like to know their shelf life,
because I fear our connection is decaying
in a dusty jar, on a lonely shelf,
somewhere back in the locked supply closet
of our middle school science classroom.
And I'm a ghost walking the halls,
footsteps echoing against green paint-chipped lockers.
I've looked in every classroom,
but I just can't seem to find
our key.

Melissa Wong, mentor

This is an excerpt from an essay I wrote recalling my kindergarten bully and the dog-eat-dog experiences that shaped my childhood in the suburbs of Chicago.

Excerpt from "Gettin' Hert"

Deshana was probably a normal-sized 6-year-old, but to me she was a 9-foot tall Amazonian woman with calf muscles the size of cantaloupes. She had the manipulating mind of a mafia don, the mouth of a prison inmate and the brute strength of a construction worker. She was a monster.

One day, Deshana was absent from kindergarten, and I craved to be her. I poked my finger into the chest of a little freckled-faced boy named Georgie and taunted, "What are you looking at, you *BLEEPIN' BLEEP?*" I had heard Deshana call me those heinous words just two days earlier. Watching him cower in my presence made me feel powerful, taller and…guilty.

The next afternoon, I made the mistake of making eye contact with her at the monkey bars. As I turned to run, her giant mutant hands pushed me to the ground, pavement careening toward my face. "*BLEEPIN' BLEEP!*" I screamed, while airborne. My forehead hit the gravel with a dull thud.

With my face wrapped in bandages, I found myself sitting silently beside her outside the principal's office. She wept. I want to tell her that I had forgiven her…that beyond her pit bull-like growl and obvious affinity for violence, we weren't so different.

Her mother – a scarier, boxier version of her daughter – arrived. She grabbed Deshana by the wrist and said, "Look at her! Look at what you did to her! Stop being a *BLEEPIN' BLEEP!*"

She yanked her into the hallway, and I heard Deshana softly whimper into the darkness.

Two days later, I returned to school and surveyed the get well cards on my desk. On the top of the heap was Deshana's. In large, semi-serial killer penmanship, the words simply read: "Sory I hert you." I believed her.

No one can say what you need to say. Be yourself in your writing— don't try to be someone else.

Brande Jackson, mentor

Crayon Thief

Purple sweatshirts. Corduroy. Garfield plastic lunch boxes. Pee. Key factors in my first year of school.

Dawn was the girl who sat next to me in kindergarten. We were seat mates.

I can't recall her last name, but it must have started with a "K" or maybe it was "Johnson," seeing as how we were in alphabetical order. I do remember that she had long, messy dark hair. And she frequently peed herself, her little plastic orange seat filling up on a fairly consistent basis, uncomfortable for both her and me.

Dawn took my crayons. I remember this with great clarity. She took all my crayons with the exception, for some reason, of the black one. Being a timid kid, non-confrontational – perhaps a budding Buddhist – I let her do so with seemingly no opposition. I simply colored with the one crayon she left me, and with pencil. I was the type of student who always did all her work and did it perfectly. This would fly out the window in the 8th grade, but for right now, in Kindergarten, I was at the very top of my academic game.

And so I had to color, to do the assignment. I like to think it was an act of resistance: "I can still color; I will simply color with what I have!" Lead & black. My teacher, Mrs. Deliah, must have thought I was a budding avant-garde artist, or perhaps a five-year-old goth.

The "Dawn Situation" continued for some time, months, unnoticed by Mrs. Deliah until some sort of crayon intervention happened, likely prompted by my mother. There was much rhetoric of 'everything is going to fine' and talk of repatriation to correct the injustice of the stolen crayons and my forced 'dark period' of Kindergarten art.

Dawn was moved to a new seat. And I don't remember who replaced her.

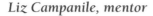

Liz Campanile, *mentor*

I'm a prose writer, but I was moved to write this poem at a WriteGirl workshop. We were given a choice of props to draw inspiration from, and I wrote this poem for my "inner child."

Prompt Poetry

Latch-hooked rugs and Holly Hobby.
Memories of January's blizzard and the start of a new decade.
A hardwood floor and mom's tea kettle coming to a boil.
Upstairs, in the walls of my lavender-colored room,
the glamour of Barbie.
Glittery disco clothes in the colors of the day –
gold, green, and purple.
The townhouse where my dolls lived had fabric swatches on its floors.

When I wanted to run and hide,
I lived in the world that was the Barbie Townhouse,
with pastel floors and plastic furniture.
Rose-colored glasses to view the days that were 5th grade.
The snow that kept me from the school play.
Christmas bells ringing without me
in the pink-tiled halls of St. Catharine's.

Deflated. My moment in the spotlight postponed indefinitely,
not knowing there wouldn't be another Christmas pageant for me.
The following year, I'd be miles away in South Florida, watching for
Santa under swaying palm trees.

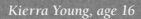

Kierra Young, age 16

*I wrote this as a journal entry during a session with my mentor.
It's about my name and how it came to be.*

Can You Say Your Doctor Named You?

The topic of my name is a touchy subject. When I was born, my mom and dad didn't have a name, so my doctor named me. And my mom and dad couldn't decide on a middle name, so they gave me two.

My full name is Kierra Amina Jeni Young. I know I came early, but I still feel like they should have had a name for me, and the fact that they thought of middle names – and not a first name – confuses me.

Not many people can say that they were named by their doctor. They have long, drawn-out stories about how they were named by their great-grandmother, who picked out their name on her deathbed.

I don't complain about my name because I like my name, and it's me. Other people have pretty bad names. Mine isn't. Sure, sometimes I feel a little left out from the rest of the world, but I realize it's another interesting life story I can share with people.

Confidence is the key
to an unlocked door.

Alicia Ruskin, mentor

I am not a parent, but through working with the girls and their families, I came to understand in a deep way the joys and challenges of parenting a girl.

going rounds

it starts with the phone, finishes with the car
in between, she finds an epic battle in a hairbrush
I get it, she's asserting her independence
throwing her skinny body against my bulk
collapsing in tears at the hint of homework or curfew
the jeans more hole than denim, the shoes
great wooden hooves
I notice she finds balance when she needs it
me the one constantly out of step
once, she and I walked for hours
through flat plains of wild grass and corn fields
her head barely grazing my shoulder
fields I had walked with my father
who vanished ahead of my metamorphosis

we were still confidantes then, her heartbreak over
a soured friendship or an unjust grade
completely within my abilities to make whole

the house traps us both
the torn cocoon watching from a high corner
the still-damp jewel, throwing herself over and
over against the windowpane

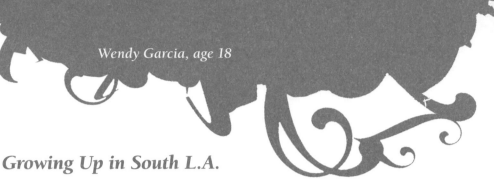

Wendy Garcia, age 18

Growing Up in South L.A.

Growing up in the south was not easy
Watching gangs fight
Helicopters and police cars swarming a house
Streets closed for investigations
Waiting to be able to go home

I realize that I want something better
I want to be able to walk without worrying
and being locked out of my house
Now that I am going to college,
I will do my best to have a better life
I want to have a program to help kids
so that instead of being in the streets,
they are playing sports or doing activities

I will improve my community
Clean up the trash and erase the graffiti
Help other kids succeed and get into college

Rachel Fain, mentor

Moving Day

Shelby sat on the floor, hugging her knees, staring blankly at the boxes when she should have been packing. Moving again – new house, new friends, new school. Her features hardened as she thought about it, mouth tightening and eyes narrowing in an effort not to cry. Standing weakly, Shelby tripped through the cardboard maze, barking her shins on the loose flaps of the unsealed cartons. She reached a pile of stuffed animals and scooped up a furry armload, ignoring the bite from the scrapes on her legs.

Unable to see the way back over Snowy and Frisky, Hephzibah and Elton, Shelby charged heedlessly into the maze. She stumbled and tumbled hard into stiff corners and rough edges, adding a bruised hip and elbow to her catalogue of injuries. She lay motionless in a heap on the floor, listening for footsteps. No one came.

Shelby started to cry, angry at the boxes, angry at herself, angry at her toys. She sat up and hurled them across the room at the waiting box. Onetwothreefour. Elton hit with a *kunk* and slid down the wall. Hephzibah and Snowy *pmphed* into the animals already packed away. Frisky made a small groaning noise as he *umphed* to the floor beside the box.

Stricken with guilt, Shelby stared over the cardboard battlements at her loyal friends. Her tears renewed and redoubled as she crashed back to the box. Blinded, she reached down and picked up the nearest toy. She was still wrapped around Frisky, the black bear's fur matted and wet, when her mother came into the room.

Cindy Collins, mentor

June, 1982

I sit alone on a rocky wall at the edge of a canyon. It's the first day of summer break and I'm here for eight weeks of freedom and adventure. The sun has set between gathering clouds and I hear the roar of buses carrying tourists out of the parking lot. For them, the show is over.

That morning, I had been given the title of "Kitchen Utility," a pair of ill-fitting black and white checked pants, a thin, white shirt three sizes too big, and an apron. A man named Squid led me to a dimly lit walk-in freezer, where globs of something red and black were frozen to the walls and floors. He handed me a knife and gave me a task: "Start scraping."

By dusk, my hands are rough and red, my hair is clumped with bits of gunk, and I smell like old lettuce. A thin line of dark ooze rings the edges of the tennis shoes crossed in my lap. At this point, it's hard to imagine where adventure will lie. I scan the shades of pink and purple melting into the greying sky and look for a sign.

Distant thunder answers me. I smell rain. The air becomes still and quiet, tinged with expectation. Feathery clouds roll in like black ink spilled in water. The sky brightens in quick bursts like a silent explosion, followed by a thunderous boom. Lightning flashes in zig-zag strikes. A wind-whipped chill blows in over a prehistoric world, bringing heavy drops that sting my face and soak my clothes. An ancient drama for me, alone. Playing nightly. I am home.

listen in on conversations-
you never know what great
story ideas you might hear.

Rachel McLeod Kaminer, mentor

I've been inspired by writing alongside my mentor, Greer. Whoops, did I say mentor? Technically, I'm the mentor and she's the mentee, but I've learned lots from our time together and have even been breaking out of my poetry comfort zone into the (frightening) world of fiction!

This Is a Piece for Me & G...

...who is sitting next to me, writing.

At this table, I forget to edit, I'm freely awkward, I ask her impulsive questions. Last night, I read where Rilke said in a letter: "We're both alone here. Let us greet one another's solitudes!" She's going to college. I try to devise writing prompts for us, but today all of my ideas are fearful – about boys or drinking or depression or body image or overachieving. Like I'm thinking up ways to save her from my own young woman mistakes. There's pink in her cheeks. It's windy out and she heard from another college. I've got choices now, she says! Yes. She has. The pink is bright and secret. She is her own young woman.

I wish she would write me a letter for when I am sixteen. I don't know what it will say, but I know what it will sound like. When G writes, it sounds like: I see the world with independent eyes. Like: I haven't experienced everything. Like: I pay attention and my guesses are good. My younger self and I listen to how thoughtfully she feels, and we feel calm. We read the writing back to G and to her older self and we're free.

None of us forget: we have choices. It's windy out. Our cheeks are pink.

Erica Logan, age 13

There's a Time

The time has come
to question the truths of this world,
but remember where I came from.

The time has come
to leave the warmth of a mother sun
and fall back on what I once knew.

The time has come
when mistakes become costly,
and, at the expense of my folly, the time has come
to grow up.

The time has come to forget the past.
Move towards the future.
Relish the present.

When freedom trumps captivity, finally there is peace.
I now have wings to live my life as it's meant to be.

4 Family

Whispered FOLK STORIES

Write when your emotion is overflowing. Experience makes all the difference in a story.

Sarah Ann Villegas, age 17

This piece was written at the WriteGirl Poetry Workshop, during the memory exercise.

Birthday

I am three.

It dangles in front of me,
Daunting, moving,
staring at me with its huge eyes.

My parents, brothers, aunt and uncle,
cousins, and grandparents tell me,
"Hit it!"

It is bigger, stronger, taller, and more colorful than me!
After hundreds of years of being beaten, smashed,
and ripped for its guts, what if
it hits me back?

I refuse.

My brother is next in line
for the piñata.

Niazayre Bates, age 14

I started this piece when I was 9, and my dad recently found it. I filled it out a little, making it more interesting and deep.

The Saddest Week

"Mommy, I feel sick," I said. "Yes, mi hija," she said quietly, "Me too." We sat there in silence while the bus bounced up and down the rocky road.

"Mommy, I don't feel sick because of Tia Marielita," I said, "I feel sick because of the bus."

Tia Mariela had been sick for weeks. Everyone knew that she was going to be leaving us soon, though no one would say so out loud. My entire family was meeting at the little hospital to be there when she passed away. It had taken three days so far to get to the little pueblo, and we were still on the way there.

"Oh, I'm sorry," she said. There was silence again while she got something out of her bag. A chicken squawked. The man next to me poked the chicken in the ribs, triggering another series of loud clucking and feathers pushing themselves through the bars of the cage.

My mom straightened back up, triumphantly holding a small bottle of pills in her hand. "What's that?" I asked.

"Here, take it. It's medicine. It'll make you feel better."

The pill crunched between my teeth and I struggled to swallow it. I grabbed the Coca-Cola in my mom's hand, eagerly gulping it down to dispel the gross taste that the pill left behind. A second later, my eyelids felt heavy and my head began to nod. I fought to keep my eyes open.

"Diana, mi hija, don't fight it." I heard mi mamá say. Her arms closed around me, preventing me from falling off the uncomfortable seat.

"Mamá..." I drifted off into a deep sleep.

Writer Words:

Don't take yourself so seriously!

Elda Pineda, mentor

This piece was written during the Fiction Workshop. The guest speaker asked us to use all of our senses to create a setting. I thought of dust and the smell of old things.

Jacob

My father Jacob calls himself a collector. Model cars, baseball cards, plaid shirts, Tupperware and newspapers. Brass animals, musical instruments, colored string, rusted tools, hundreds of baggies full of buttons. Jars of "lucky" pennies cover the mantle. Stacks of dusty *National Geographics* wobble and threaten to topple over. There is never anyplace to sit. The last time I visited, maybe four years ago, we stood awkwardly in the kitchen, between piles of unopened mail and half-eaten dinners. "Dad, maybe some weekend Daniel and I can come over and help you tidy up?" It wasn't until after I said it that I realized the ridiculousness of the offer. One weekend. Tidy up.

I poked at a crate full of mismatched silverware. "What use could you possibly have for this stuff, Dad!" It was impossible to keep the frustration out of my voice when what I really wanted to say was, "I'm afraid you're going to die here – that you won't be able to get to the phone. That the paramedics won't be able push back the pile of my high school soccer trophies and old ballet shoes to get the gurney through. That you'll trip on a mound of books and you'll fall and break your hip and..."

He looked at me for a long time from behind his smudged reading glasses and sighed heavily. "But they're not things, baby bird. They're memories."

Kirsten Giles, mentor

This poem was inspired by my trips to see my sister in Minnesota.

A Trip to the Country

I arrive at the airport and stand by the baggage carousel,
waiting for my sample-sized toiletries, and wrinkle-resistant layers.

Outside on the curb, my breath is like chalk dust in the Midwestern air.
I'm waiting for my sister, who helped me tie my shoes,
who taught me how to read.

She arrives in her rugged truck, mud caked on the fenders,
the smell of work and children, her hair
long, straight and clean.

When she smiles at me, I see an old reflection,
patent leather shoes and tangled pigtails.
I forget the 405, the conference calls, the deadlines.
The echoing concrete seasons.

Her house is like an old coat. Worn shoes, mittens
held together with a string.
A familiar scrapbook of places and names.
Our grandmother's blanket. Our father's photographs.

At night, she brings me a small electric fan.
Because she knows I can't sleep in the silence.
It's like cotton in my ears.

Emily Trang, age 17

As Vietnam War refugees, my parents have been through very hard times. Although it is difficult to capture their strength and courage, I felt Haiku would do.

Dark Night

Tet, the day for joy
What should be filled with fortune
Is instead blood red

All refugees know
that day. It makes them shudder
and close their eyes

Villages attacked
Killing thousands, killing peace
and serenity

Families fleeing
for their dear lives, crying as
they lose their loved ones

He still has nightmares
Fear of death by communists
Dad, all is okay

Ba Noi* recounts
of her hardened life to the
child who listens

Child tucked away
She stares out with forlorn eyes
Tears in the dark night

*Ba Noi means "grandmother" in Vietnamese.

in scene writing,
there is power
in the silences.

Maria Flores, age 17

I made this for my little brother at the Poetry Workshop – we were told to write about a childhood memory and my brother's birth is number one.

Amorcito

"Ya nació tu hermanito!"
I heard in the middle of the night
When I was four
And a little boy for me to love was born.

Thirteen years later,
I clearly remember
holding him in my arms,
the little boy of a day.

My Amorcito! My little love!
Someone new for me to love.

He cried and cried when they took him from me.
Half asleep, what did he want?
His bottle, a change, our mother, what?
"Hold him so we can call the nurse!" our father told me.

He stopped his protest
when we felt each other's warmth.
He wanted me!
But why? Could it be?
My Amorcito! My little love!
Loved me as much as I loved him?

His little smile said it all.

Ashlee Polarek, age 18

I began writing childhood memories as a small project and most of them turned out to be about my great-grandfather, Popie.

Popie

I remember going to the cemetery with Popie. He would bring stale bread for me to feed the ducks. I would stand on a bridge, tossing the crumbs to the hungry mallards. He would wait until every morsel was dispersed.

I remember Popie picking me up from school. We would journey to McDonald's for my favorite gourmet meal, Chicken McNuggets and ice cream, and then head to the arcade where he let me waste his money.

I remember a small blue bouncy ball. I would run to Popie's silver mailbox and toss it in, slamming the door, telling him he had to wait for it to cook. He teased me and tried to open it against my vehement protests, but waited until I told him the ball was done.

I remember Popie's white well-worn Grand Marquis. Popie would sing to the rhythm of the windshield wipers, as they cleared the curtain of rain. "Windshield wipers go swish swish."

I remember our backyard jungle in Azusa. Popie and I would brandish palm fronds, like natives in the Amazon, chanting, "A Booma Boom" repeatedly to the neighboring Glendora tribe.

How I wish I had a time machine to relive those moments again.

Jane Anderson, mentor

During the objects exercise at the Fiction Workshop, one of the volunteers held up a sad-looking pillow with a butterfly on it that looked handmade. I wondered, who in the world would make such a thing?

Handmade in Iowa

She knew what her daughter was thinking the moment she gave her the pillow: "Tacky." She could see her daughter's eyes go a little flat before she said, "Oh, thanks, Mom."

She knew that butterflies were not really her daughter's taste, but she had loved them when she was a little girl. Butterfly stickers, butterfly hair clips, butterfly sheets…oh, her daughter couldn't get enough of them back then, and she had loved purple and pink, too. "Oh, Mommy, I want to wear my pink tights with the purple top!"

But now – oh well. People change. Her daughter lives in New York. Her apartment has very little clutter, and everything is in beige and greys. On the walls are black and white photos that were taken by someone important. But there are no people in the pictures – just buildings and sky and empty streets. Not a sign of life in any of them, except for the one where if you look very closely you can see a bird on a telephone wire. There is an expensive-looking couch that is low and straight and not very comfortable and that is where her daughter politely places the pillow. But she knows that it will end up in the closet so as not to clash with the greys.

What on earth was she thinking when she picked out the colors of the yarn, the pattern with the butterflies? She was thinking that her daughter needed one thing, just one thing that was made with love.

Mia Feagin, age 16

The Sweet Sensation of a Mother

I've watched her grow just as she's watched me grow. I've watched the way she walks, talks, and carries herself. I try to be just like her.

It had to be a hard task being a single parent with a child like me, but I've watched her make it. I'd wake up seeing a beautiful smile on her face and end my day seeing that same smile. I remember her raspy voice and the advice she gave me that still rumbles through my head.

Wonderful Sundays, feet kicked up, lights dimmed down, *Law and Order* flashing before my eyes. Bad hair days when she was the only one coming to my rescue. Nights when she worked her butt off, then took me to my activities, and still took college classes. When I walked onstage, with bright lights shining on my face and butterflies in my stomach, one look at her face in the audience took all the fears away.

She's given me guidance and stability. She inspires me and brings positive energy into my life. On the days I think I can't make it, I take one look at her photo and the strong woman who pushed through many obstacles. She got me where I am today.

Sometimes I call her Mom, sometimes I call her Mommy. Anytime I call her, I know she'll be there for me. It's the sweet sensation of a mother that can take a child far beyond the stars.

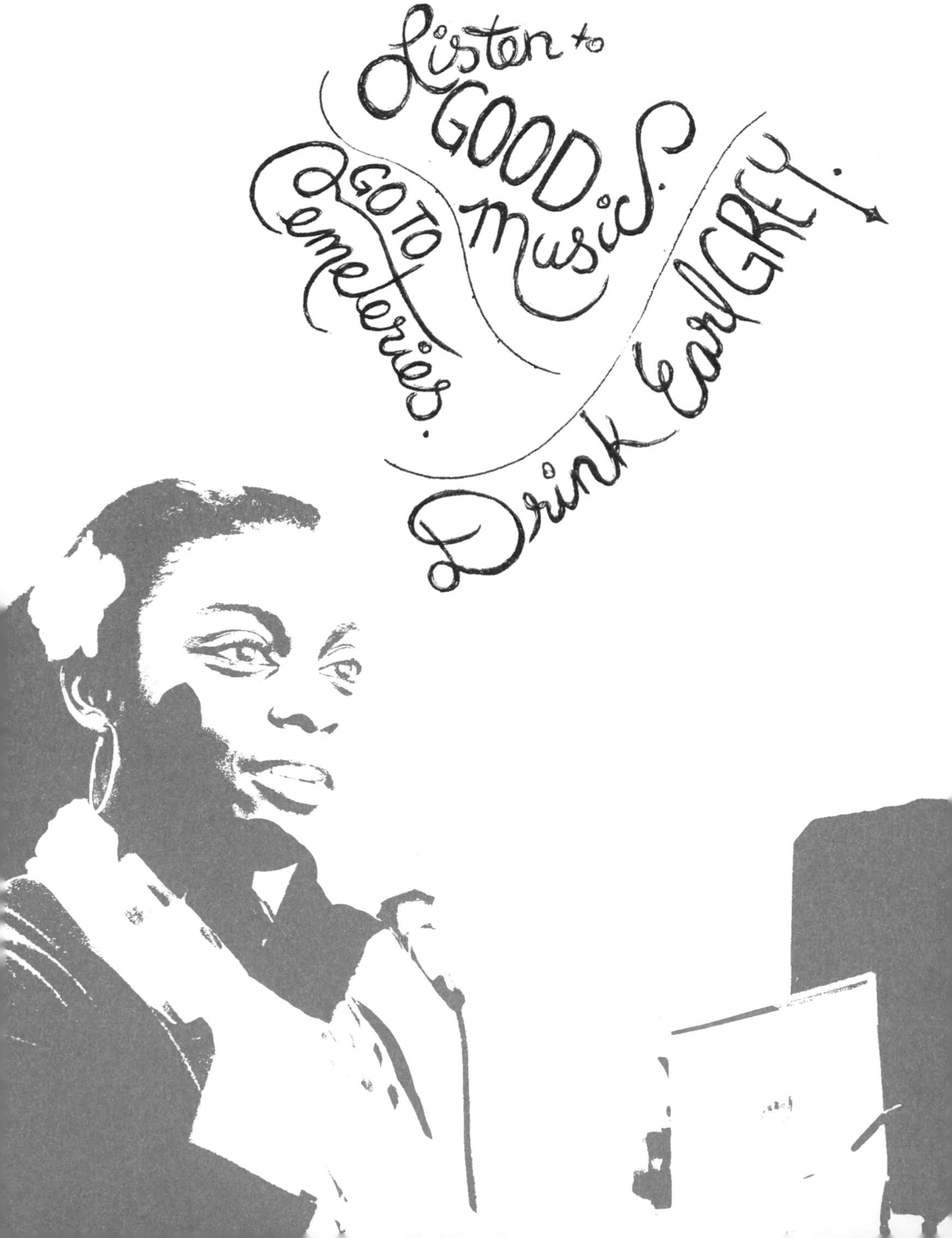
Listen to GOOD Music.
GO TO Cemeteries.
Drink Earl GREY!

Krista Gelev, age 15

Written at the WriteGirl Poetry Workshop, this is a medley of childhood memories derived from rainy summer afternoons in Bulgaria.

Afternoon Inside

Inky heaps of sky
Scarlet jams bubble on an ancient stove
Whispered folk stories bounce upon our wooden cave
While crisp, smoldering embers, like fairies, enchant us
Cocooned by the unbroken murmuring of rain and
Wrapped in moth-nibbled blankets, old and young melt
As we are lulled by a grandmother's hum

5 FANTASY & WHIMSY

SaFe
FrOM
SNApPING
JaWS

Lyla Matar, age 14

I wrote this when I was struggling with certain situations that were going on. I tried to write about the "game" that was going on in my head.

The Game of Sir and Knight

The bell. Banking customs,
falling fancy. Flatter, simplicity, divinity,
all swimming in the sea of pinnacles that seem to appear out of air.
Sir Something. Knight No One.
Both bowing, conscious yet unaware in approach to reality,
afraid to wake the children. The creator, finding, found
awash in the everlasting slight of playing cards.
Playing with Sir Something, Knight No One.

A table set with men. Tabula Rasa.
Slipping and crunching conversation,
wonders for the ear to stumble on,
such things the likes of which plain men have not heard.

All the while, Sir Something, Knight No One,
tipping hats, scales, and words.
Fools, and children of nothing but the earth,
bemusing men, an endeavor of discovery.
A golden bemusing of culture.
The inept chaotic reformation,
something along the lines of humanity.

Sir Something. Knight No One.
Betting on the game that will never end…
that has never been played.

DO NOT

ANY WORK.
YOU WILL REGRET
THE DECISION LATER.

Woaria Rashid, age 17

*When I finished reading "The Metamorphosis" by Franz Kafka,
I tried to imitate a page of Kafka's writing.*

The Transfiguration

When Clyde Oliver woke up one morning from unsettling dreams,
he found himself changed in his bed into a dying phoenix. He was
lying on his back, and when he lifted his head a little, he saw his
ashy crimson belly and deteriorating fiery plumage as it lay limply
on his bedspread.

"What's happened to me?" he thought. It wasn't a dream. His room,
a human room, although a little too small, lay peacefully between
its four familiar walls.

Clyde reached for his glasses on top of the Pembroke table beside
his bed – which then, he realized that wings replaced his fingers. As
he lay on the bed, listening to the heavy raindrops pattering on the
ground, he felt a sensation of overwhelming despair sharply strike
him in remembrance of the hopes he had after graduating from a
prestigious university…only to find his way back to his parents' home.

The alarm rang at 6:00 a.m., time for work. He attempted to hit
the snooze button, but his wings knocked it to the floor, which
unfortunately did not disintegrate, but instead continued to play
the cacophonous tone. "I'll simply sleep for a few more minutes so
this nightmare will be over," he thought, but that was completely
impracticable. No matter how hard he tried to wake from this
incubus, he simply could not, and was almost falling off his scanty
single-sized bed. He gave up and cried out in delirium.

He heard his mother's footsteps walking towards his room, and
shortly after, a sharp knock rapped three times on the door.
"Clyde," she called out. "It's half-past six, you'll be late for work."
Clyde was shocked to hear his broken, hoarse voice struggling to
form words, but responded with a soft cry, which simultaneously
sounded like a soft song. Instantaneously, his mother opened the
door wide open, only to see, in her disbelief, Him.

Amanda Elend, mentor

I wrote this at the WriteGirl Poetry Workshop during an exercise in which we turned a description of a happy memory from childhood into a poem.

Living

"Alligator's coming," he said.
I knew what to do.
Jump to the living room couch, safe from snapping jaws.
Over the stained cushions, through the piano bench, to the
loveseat we go.
Touch the ground, and he'll have you for dinner.

Just a game. And real. And not.
Dad's tickle fingers ready to bite.

"Alligator's coming," I said.
But girls grow, couches sag.
Pianos break.

A room for living.
My brother and his girlfriend, kissing.
Alligator, coming.

In the next room,
the glass frame in the hall
shows shadows, kissing.
There, but not. But there.

The living room:
where a girl and her brother
might get bit.

inhale
your
thoughts,

exhale
your
characters.

Eva Joan Robles, age 15

I wrote this based on a dream I had right after a WriteGirl workshop.

Wondering Dreams

Lost in an unknown land with nowhere to go, I wonder what to do with the smell of roses. I feel my stomach grumbling, and I'm walking and walking and so tired. Everything is so black, with nothing to see. The sounds of wild animals surround me. There is no one to protect me or keep me company. It's so cold. What is this land?

Suddenly, everything is white. There is nowhere to go and everything looks the same. I hear intense echoes when I speak and an enormous silence too. What shall I do? In the corner of my eye, I see the light. I believe it will take me where I won't be scared any longer.

As I run to it, I see a man who seems familiar. He looks identical to my grandfather who died before I was born. I have only seen him in pictures. He tells me he loves me and to never go the wrong way in life. I am frightened and I begin to cry.

It was just a dream.

Jennifer Ayuso, age 17

After the WriteGirl Character and Dialogue Workshop, I wrote this monologue from the perspective of a character who encounters the ghost of someone they once knew.

Ghost

Why? Why do you put yourself through this pain?
Please, I beg of you,
say something, anything
for silence is a cold-hearted death.

Leave me –
You'll be normal again.
Go live your life.

I'd rather drag the dagger
over my own grief-stricken heart
than bear the thought of never seeing you again.

We all hold on to pointless memories,
but you just happen to be
the one I can't let go of.

I'll remain faithful, no matter
that my heart is shattered,
twisted, and bent.
"Love is in so many ways,"
it said with a smile.

Leaving fears behind
soaring in the lightless air.
A reason: to rise, to live, to die.

Gracefully you come near.
"Let us not shed tears,
for my time was long overdue."

Peggy Marrin Johnson, mentor

I wanted to focus on the power of words and how expressing oneself is, like breathing, a holy act.

In the Beginning...

I take the word inside my mouth
like a communion wafer   it feels bland
I roll it over under around my tongue   cheek it
it sticks to my palate
until my wily tongue
pries it gently from the roof
Slowly, ever so slowly
it slides, slips and starts   to dissolve
its effervescence EXPLODING
in a shower of tingles
Shooting down my throat
and past the epiglottis
Entering the place where the
breath of life resides

I do not choke on   the word
as it brushes over cilia
pushing along to the air sacs
Through the alveoli
And gassy residue

it streaks back up my lungs   until
poised on the tip of my tongue
I SHOUT it out.

Lorren Verrett, age 16

I wrote this at the Fiction Workshop, using objects that were placed around the room for inspiration. I focused on a pretty masquerade mask.

The Man in the Mask

The moon hung high in the sky above the Eiffel tower like a flat, silver hat. Stars decorated the Paris cityscape. A light summer breeze carried the scents of freshly baked bread and women's perfumes.

He took a step forward, approaching the end of the alley, where she sat on a chipped yellow bench, waiting for the bus. He hadn't seen anyone lovelier than her before. Her features were so perfect. Her light brown skin was void of any marks or scars, hair as black as pitch, tumbling down her smooth shoulders in perfectly coiled ringlets. Her eyes – how achingly breathtaking they were! – dark and twinkling, with a light older than time itself.

She waited at the bus stop in front of this alley every day. He didn't know why, or perhaps, for whom. All he knew about her was that she would take him willingly. Like the Phantom of the Opera, he wore a mask to cover the flaws of his countenance. It was nothing fancy, since nothing of any considerable value should touch such a repulsive face. No, just a simple black mask with two round holes cut out to allow him to lay his dull green gaze upon her.

He was so close to the end of alley now that the shadows of the surrounding apartment buildings no longer concealed his petite physique. Blonde bangs falling into his face, the masked man crept closer to the woman, until he was directly behind her. She was immersed in her cell phone. She didn't seem to feel his presence. God, she was so beautiful, worthy of the love of a prince.

"How I would love for you to be my princess."

She turned around.

Don't Let your inner voice STIFLE your creative voice.

Lauren Davila, age 16

Roger Sherman Loomis, a medieval scholar, suggested that "Cavalon" was a corruption of "Avalon." I chose this name to show the fall from perfection into destruction.

Cavalon

Her laugh breaks the silence,
Permeating through the broken castle,
Filling the space left behind by the settling dust.

She walks over and around bloodstained stones,
Cracked glass splintering
Underneath her mud-covered slippers,
Broken armor and swords lie on the ground,
Forgotten in the pandemonium.

She twists her ankle on a golden object.
Looking down, she picks it up
And places it triumphantly on her head.

She strides purposefully toward the intact throne.
Sitting down, she surveys the room, the palace,
The utter destruction she has wrought.
Her time has come.

Fate had prophesied her downfall, her death,
But even fate can be wrong. Even fate can be changed.
She closes her eyes and revels in her victory.

Her reign has begun, and this time,
There is no one to get in her way.

Tasha Caday, age 13

Alpacalypse

There was absolutely no warning that she would bring it home. An alpaca. But not just any alpaca. A bright, blindingly pink one.

"But why, Lola, why?" I cried. "We have no space for an alpaca!" My grandmother shrugged with an unsure smile.

My sister – the married one, with the wanna-be gangster husband who enjoys long walks and playing "Loving You" on his boom system – screamed from the bathroom and ran out fuming. "Lola, your alpaca just got Charlie covered in… in… *tae*!" Charlie is her adorable little Maltese puppy, and *tae* is Tagalog for, well, poop. "There are these weird purple, plastic bits in it, too!" she added.

My face contorted into something grim and serious. I exclaimed, "Where are my purple rain boots?"

I marched into the bathroom with my grandmother scrambling after me. Yup. Those were my boots alright. I turned, ready to curse profanities at it furiously and tirelessly, but I simply stepped back, stunned. It was… *purple*. The same shade as my boots. "What… the what?"

the ink's not dry

6 Writing & Inspiration

Zoe Lawrence, age 15

I based this on "The Love Song of J. Alfred Prufrock," as well as on our cold world, tied together by microchips and caffeine.

Love and the Dormant Fast Lane

There is always a fear of the highway giving out
of the neon drying up
of memories misremembered
dismembered

of disturbing dormant universes
measuring out your life in text messages
status updates
frappuccino straws.

The hardest thing about writing is simply to <u>do it.</u>

DO IT!

India Radfar, mentor

Us

here we are, sitting around
three tables together
pens and journals all a scatter
on top

here we are
bags on our shoulders, backpacks on our backs
no one puts anything down

then pens begin moving, heads bend
to the page under cornrows, topknots
or bangs low to the eye
also hair loose and long, beautiful waves of
hair

pens keep moving, nail polish
flashing cherry red, shiny green,
also black and tomato red

soon we stretch and the backpacks come off our backs
our burdens slide to the floor
where they belong

and we, somber and smiling, tattooed or not
sitting here,

we write

Sarah Tuibeo, age 17

A Tribute to My Pen

This is for all the pens
They were there for me
When people were not

Not the slightest clue what I would do
Without my pens or any other marking device
To record my deepest thoughts, my most artistic work
Not to mention, the honor of recording
My most random ideas and
My mind vomit

My pens have been lost
My pens have been dropped
There are times when they have run out of ink
Like when I'm writing the climax
So disappointing to me

Regardless of these pen malfunctions
It's more than a blessing to have pens
I can record anything, anytime, any day
We're a team, that's how we roll
Like that ballpoint pen on the floor

learn a little bit
a lot about
of things.

Inez Singletary, mentor

This piece was written in a WriteGirl workshop. The prompt was to describe an object in detail, then write about it.

My First Journal

It was a small book with a white "leather" padded cover that was labeled, "Autographs," in gilded letters. The pages were pastels of pink, blue and green. It had a little lock and key. It was standard for us high school graduates to have such a book to collect the autographs and comments of our friends.

But I wasn't very interested in having other people write in my book. To me, the book said, "Write in me. Tell me your thoughts. Write what you would say if you could, if you weren't afraid or shy. Write down what you see, what you feel, what you remember and what you don't want to forget. Write it down and lock it up when you are finished." The lock seemed to tell me that this was the place for secrets, for guts and heart. I worried a little that someone might read what I wrote for only my own eyes to witness. They could probably break into it if they wanted to.

In the end, it did not really matter that someone might know my private thoughts. It mattered that I put those secret thoughts down as a way to talk to myself, know myself, to let myself in on what was important to me. It was important that I unlock my tongue and speak in script, read it again later and know.

I read it to my own daughter when she graduated from high school. It didn't sound profound. It sounded a little silly, especially when I wrote about my first love, who would later be her father.

She wanted to keep the book. I let her.

Shaze Williams, age 17

Two Writers Talk About Negativity: A Dialogue

Jas: I have no idea why things keep happening the way they do, nor do I know why it keeps playing in my mind…I was just so happy last night. Maybe I *am* insane.

Nol: Like I said, everyone's insane, and insanity comes on many different levels. Since you can talk about your insanity, it's probably not bad – or serious.

Jas: That's good.

Nol: It *is* good. See? Try asking yourself questions.

Jas: How will I answer? I don't really know myself.

Nol: Get to know yourself.

Jas: It's not like I can take myself on a date or anything.

Nol: You're making this too difficult. Besides, you and I are writers, and through writing we have pieces of ourselves – just read your own writing.

Jas: My writing is not good. No one pays attention to it.

Nol: Your writing is awesome, so hush.

Jas: You always say that.

Nol: Because it is. I remember failing at writing a Shakespearean sonnet. I finally conquered it, and you know I can be even more depressing than Edgar Allan Poe. You exceed your limits, and then there are new ones. But really there are no limits for writers.

Jas: Pfft, I can beat you!

Nol: There ya go, Jas, that's the spirit.

WRITE ABOUT THINGS YOU **WANT** TO KNOW ABOUT BUT DON'T UNDERSTAND.

Ashaki M. Jackson, *mentor*

I wrote this for my mentee, Ciara Blackwell, in celebration of her last year with WriteGirl. It is a letter written in an experimental style that plays on sound and space. I trust that she will use her potential to shed light for her generation and others.

Articulation

Girl,

From here on, you will not remember origins. They will steep in old teacups like certain potions. Even these words did not exist before this statement; they are just as new as the sounds

ern   alk   ool

No past – there is only you and your momentum breaking the sky. May your words break the world in lovely ways *[crr aaaa   k sssss]*. Dear Girl,

        This letter is cracked.

From here on, your paths mend and beget maps. Your questions beget philosophers. You name all animals in the kingdom. You begin days.

Tell us the tastes of joy.

Tell us the difference between a white page
                and snow.

Victoria Tsou, age 17

During one of our writing sessions, my mentor, Inez, gave me the idea of writing on the topic of why we love to write. This piece came directly from the heart.

I Write Because

I write because my hand can get it out when my mouth won't let it out. Writing unties the tongue. My handwriting is my utensil to paper. Typing on the computer stifles my thoughts.

I like to write because even when I feel ill at ease, I want to share my thoughts and feelings. I can fix my writing with edits, and then I can read it fairly smoothly.

Speaking can fluster me. If a stranger approaches me, my tongue can shrivel up, and I may talk in a strained tone. Sometimes, my face will turn red, too. With writing, I can take my time to find the correct word that I can't always think of when I'm talking.

During English class, we wrote essays involving the use of specific vocabulary. My class noticed that the stories I wrote were funny, even though I don't really appear to be a funny type of person.

Writing is fun! I compose stories in my mind that my nerves would otherwise stumble over when speaking. Writing allows me to keep a long-term record of my ideas.

Greer Silverman, age 18

I wrote this piece during a meeting with my mentor, Rachel. I wanted to express a very specific feeling and I kept coming back to the same line – "the ink's not dry."

Sheets

Hair clings to my neck like cold sweat, the ink's not dry.
I put the sheets out the window, to let them
snap themselves in the damp. Hours later I find them, papers
yellow and gray with dirt from the steam and smoke from the streets.
The ink's not dry.

Why. Why would you say that.
(What made you stay quiet all those weeks before?)
...Slick stones, old paint warmed over in the evening,
the coffee spoons bent along the table,
and the stillborn words...

The ink's not dry. I stare out across the bloated sky
between the cracks in the table, the chips in my fingernails.
I thought there was something in the air, some flies
murmuring above our heads, mocking themselves
against the window screens.

Try writing by candlelight.

InVitATIoN for INSPIRATION

Tiffany Tsou, age 16

I wrote this piece at the Poetry Workshop. I tried to write about all the things that I was willing to do for my muse!

Dear Artsy Abigail

Dear Artsy Abigail,

In the current Dark Days of the school year, I'm having trouble with my art final. The task is to create a meaningful masterpiece, and as usual, my ideas are boring. As I was browsing through "Inspiration Tribune," I came across your ad. You instantly stood out to me among the other ads. Maybe it was your hairstyle, or funny email address, I don't know.

I need your help. You were awarded "Most Inspirational" in 2009! Truly amazing! Will you come inspire my art? Here at my home, you'll be completely pampered, cleaned, fed, and entertained. Unlimited luxuries: unlinted clothes, squeezed toothpaste on your toothbrush, cracked hard-boiled eggs, repainted chipped nails, pre-warmed bed before you sleep, and I'll even pay for your unlimited texting. Honestly, you'll want to stay with me forever. I'm not bad company either, with a winning sense of style and unmatched humor. You'll love me and you'll find out why! Hope to hear from you soon!

Love,
Tiffany

BREATHE LIFE INTO A CHARACTER - GIVE THEM A VOICE AND A VERY SPECIFIC PAIR OF SHOES. DETAILS MAKE A CHARACTER LIVE.

Danielle Flores, age 15

How Do I Lasso My Muse?

She prefers chocolate
Men with abs
Tickles to get out of bed
Gone for days
Far away
Returns empty yet filled with stories

In a meadow she lies
The sun in her face
Flowers fall around her

Visions of Wyoming and cowboys fill her head
How do I lasso my muse?
When she stands ready to battle with my ego.

Shakira Ellis, age 15

This is a poem about my muse.

She Makes Me Write

She makes me write.

With a burning desire, and the beauty of her spirit,
she sets my heart afire.

She makes me write.

A lily in her hair,
pure calm in her fury.

She makes me write,
a rainbow where she steps, a soft light in her eyes.

She makes me write.

Use all your senses —
be specific and describe what
you want your reader to
experience.

Zoe Lawrence, age 15

This was written at the Poetry Workshop. I finally reconciled my two muses – my Fair Youth and Dark Lady, if you will – and if they can stop fighting for my brain long enough to stay in the same poem, life will be good.

Two Muses

My muse was once tall and fire-haired,
    passion embodied,
   courted only with tears and supplication,
  and low-calorie sweeteners,
watching Firefly,
smelling of tea tree and overscented soap.

She left in September in search of a sadder life,
   and a better therapist.

My new muse is six-foot-one and a half,

   dressed in black wool,
    unwittingly inspiring.

Valerie Iwamoto, age 15

It feels good to let everything out on a piece of paper.

My Muse

to unravel the misery
find the source of darkness
you ask for forgiveness
taking the indigo smoke
twisting its insides
into the most glowing
efficient light

Don't be afraid to start over from scratch if you don't **love** what you've written.

Kylie Krueger, age 13

Sharing the Muse

She walks.
Follows me.
Sure, we are friends.
She is my inspiration.
The hope behind my words.

She is always here.
Her suggestions,
her ideas drive me.

Sometimes we talk
about nothing,
about everything.

I ask her,
"You've been here this whole time?
Do you not have another?"
"I do."

Soon I awake
to find she has gone.
She left me, for her other.

McKenzie Givens, age 16

This piece was written during our Poetry Workshop, as part of an exercise in writing about the muse and how she presents herself to you.

Pulling Back the Curtain

This is an open invitation for inspiration.

Lend me your eyes, and I'll give you my voice.
I'll give you my tongue, swirling with anticipation
at the sight of a particularly brutal sunrise
tearing open the sky for all to see.

Lend me your ears, and I'll translate pieces
of overheard conversation
into extemporaneous musings
on the creation of destruction
or punctuate declarations of love
with a slap in the face.

Lend me your hands, and I'll show you the universe.
I'll show you a myriad of constellations, infinite in nature,
reflected in the finite dust of your translucent flesh.

Lend me your tongue, and I'll welcome you into my temple,
this holiest of altars, torn open by the beasts of poetry
as blood mixed with flame mixed with ink
pours onto the page and clears space for new growth.

Lend me your body, and I'll walk you through this city.
This city paved with a mosaic of sincere hypocrisies,
hidden histories, and honest delusions.
I'll take you to the places where we are born, die, and live impatiently.

Lend me your time, and I'll illuminate the darkest of prisons
with unadulterated revolution.

Anything and everything can be a story idea. search for inspiration everywhere!

Kai McDaniel, age 15

At the Poetry Workshop, we were encouraged to write a poem about our muse and how we would court it. I found the topic very inspiring.

Courting My Muse

An annoyance at times
and a treasure at others.

To court my muse,
I must acknowledge
the new form it takes every day.
I gawk at its presence.

Loving the attention,
it sits down with me, next to me,
always caringly wrapping its arms around me,
quietly listening.

My muse lets me tell it all,
my daily thoughts and wonders.
My muse tells me
when it's my time
to gain the attention and gather resolve.

Heather Lim, age 13

"Yes" was the answer

I'd humbly ask her to stay
in my crummy art studio.
When "yes" was the answer, she'd
Be the motivation for my perfect picture of life.
She'd dance in a summer dress,
Her giggles jingling like bells.
Her light smile warming
My sullen days.

Dory Graham, age 16

I've struggled with my muse my whole life, and the concept of a muse is enthralling.

Her Demands

In truth, I don't court my muse at all.

That's probably why I've felt

the sting of her revenge

and known the emptiness of her absence.

Draw what you feel, my art teacher says.

Well,

what if I can't feel anything?

The deepest terror

from the ultimate accursed thought.

I guess I don't court my muse, really.

But I do know what she wants.

She wants

the splash of color.

She wants

the stark reality of print

and she demands

that I be her slave.

She wants me to devote my whole self to her,

to spend my life studying, laboring towards improvement.

But I don't.

I accept the frustration

of the gap between my ideas and my abilities,

the wasting of time and potential.

Because, what if I'm not ready?

fold, straIghteN, TwIST, Turn

Surrounded by Symbols

A symbol is a physical representation of an object, idea or relationship. Its purpose is to convey meaning in the same way a heart may represent love, or a light bulb may symbolize an idea.

Symbol Experiments:

1. What are some symbols that you can think of? Where do you see symbols in everyday life around you? In your journal, draw a symbol that you have seen and then write a poem about it. Write about what the symbol is trying to tell you – what secret meaning it holds.

2. Kate Johannesen, in her poem, "Maze," was inspired by the image of a Celtic knot as a symbol. (If you don't know what a Celtic knot is, great! Use your imagination and describe what you picture it to be. There are no wrong answers!) What are some of the things that the knot symbolizes to her? Choose a symbol, perhaps one associated with a culture or a group, and write a free association poem about whatever comes to your mind. **Challenge:** Use a thesaurus to replace at least one word in your poem with a word you might not have used otherwise.

3. A symbol gets beyond the literal meaning of a word or object. For example, think of a campfire and all the ways a campfire could symbolize family, friendship, community, illumination of ideas and hope for the future. Choose an ordinary object. What could it symbolize, beyond its obvious use? Get very specific and very detailed. Write two paragraphs or more. **Challenge:** Use 3 metaphors in your writing.

Ruby Pineda, age 14

One of the stations at the Poetry Workshop inspired me to write this poem. It is for the ones I love when they feel down and confused.

Dancing Moon

When all alone, down and grey
And everyone is elsewhere
Just dance like the moon is watching
For the moon will always know how to waltz

Kate Johannesen, age 17

At the Poetry Workshop, I was inspired by the symbolic image of a Celtic knot, and I wrote this as a train-of-thought piece.

The Maze

A knotted mind,
a tangle of confusion and sentences run together, words
lose meaning as sounds bend sharply around corners in the
endless maze of thought, the
knot is complex, but through it all,
unity.

Symmetry.

There is a certain peace to be found following the walls,
caressing the edges, coloring inside the lines,
infinitely.

Without making any sense at all.

Grace Ardolino, age 14

I wrote this poem during the WriteGirl Poetry Workshop, inspired by the traditional yellow and black hazard symbol.

Toxic

The air stirs, dry and amber,
she dances in circles, twirls her fingers in her hair.
Forever I could wait here.
Wait for her to see me watching,
wanting her to love the world right back to me.
She throws her arms in the air, falls in the snow.

I feel like I know her, as if I could be gifted
with her name, but I…
know better.
She is a hazard, and as soon as she would come,
she would disappear.
Even now she leaves me to wait,
the sight of her eyes making me ache,
yet it's still too late for me to fall.
(I would have broken myself for her anyway.)

My heart, fair-skinned and easily burned
by the heat of disappointment.
No, I could never fall like this,
Because I would know better than to love.

WRITE IN **45**-MINUTE INCREMENTS. IT'LL HELP YOU KEEP YOUR ENERGY UP WITHOUT INTERRUPTING THE FLOW.

Synesthesia

Synesthesia is a neurological condition in which a person's senses get mixed up; one might, for example, experience sounds as colors. As writers, we try to use all of our senses to enrich our writing. But what if we use our senses to describe things that can't actually be experienced in that way? For example, joy looks like an acrobat flying through the air trailing bright streamers.

Make sense? Try these:

- What does moonlight taste like?

- What does childhood smell like?

- What does the color turquoise feel like?

- What does sadness look like?

- What do poppies sound like?

- What does anticipation smell like?

- What does anger taste like?

- What does truth feel like?

- What does love sound like?

Now make up some of your own.
Pick your favorite phrase and use it as the basis for a longer piece. Or, combine several into one poem or story.

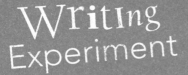

Writing Experiment

Cassie Shima, age 15

My mentor Rachel and I were talking about synesthesia, and she asked me to write what sadness looks like, and so I did.

Ice Cream: A Tragedy

The boy looked up out of his hole in the sand. He heard something – the merry music of the painted truck danced lazily in the air. He saw it materialize before him, a swirling menagerie of yellow and orange. He crawled out of the hole, and raced towards it, practically tripping over every grain of sand before landing in line for the sun-bleached wonder truck.

Anxiety bubbled inside him, starting from the pit of his stomach to the tip of his tongue. He tasted its lemon-lime acidity, the bitter sting of crunchy nails. He looked around at the grinning children, happy tongues licking Technicolor ice cream that dripped slowly down their sandy wrists. He could not bear the jealous pain he felt in his chest.

He was third from the grimy window, and excitement crept between his toes. It crawled up his foot and twisted around his calf. He tried jumping, in the hope that this would send it back to the hot sand – it worked. He was so close, he could smell the milky sweetness of the rainbow of flavors that waited inside the truck. He walked up to the tiny window and ordered strawberry ice cream on a waffle cone with a maraschino cherry. The rich taste of artificial fruit covered his tongue in a symphony of sweet victory!

The boy was so enthralled by his new frosty companion that he failed to notice the concrete curb and fell to his knees with an agonizing thud. A small crowd of seagulls gathered around him, fighting for the shattered bits of waffle cone strewn across a growing puddle of pink. He turned back toward the ice cream truck, only to find its tail lights driving obliviously away. The boy scowled at the sticky pink remains of his melting glory and wept.

write in WHATEVER MOOD you're in. Be open to seeing where your writing leads you.

Odes

An ode is a poem or a song of praise addressed to someone or something, naming their wonderful qualities. Some of the most famous poems in history are odes. It's one of those forms that feels serious at first, but is perfect for playfulness: Melissa Wong's poem "Oh Kindle" is a great example of an ode that turns into an ironic, backhanded compliment.

Odes can be written for heroes and leaders, underdogs and outcasts. You could write an ode to flip flops, or a storage closet. Who are the people or objects in your everyday life that you would like to highlight with a tribute poem? **Challenge:** Write an ode, no longer than one page, that does not mention the item or person you are describing. Let the reader see or smell or hear the subject of your ode through your specific details.

Melissa Wong, mentor

There is nothing like browsing a bookstore and stumbling across a book you didn't know you wanted. I wrote this piece after using an eReader for the first time.

Oh Kindle

Oh Kindle
Your buttons are so cold
Your words so lifeless
Your face so shiny but still –
What is this I see?
A slight expression of snobbery?
Page up, page down, power off
You are not the boss of me, robot.

I yearn for those smudged pages
Those that tear, fold and cut
Deep into my fingertips
Those thick spines that crease
Under the pressure of my eager palms
The musty scent of aged pulp and ink
Burning my pointed nose
A nose buried deep in its stories.

Ellen Girardeau, mentor

At a friend's house, I slept in her college-age daughter, Julia's, bedroom. Julia is a writer and avid reader, as her specially built wall-to-ceiling bookshelf showed. When I asked if Julia ever read digital books, her mother laughed. "Never," she answered, "she is against them."

Shelf Shocked

Drop the digital tablet in water
and you will be shocked
to see the 100-odd books you stored
inside, like dry, flat, colorless sponges

spring to vivid, tactile, perfect-bound life,
marginalia and bent pages still intact,
smudged paragraphs suggesting seaside summers,
smoky campfires, lavender bubble baths –

the comforting weight restored,
the well-read volumes suddenly visible,
solid in your hand

Random Inspiration

Inspiration is all around you. As a writer, once you start to observe the signs, objects, people, conversations, symbols, animals, sounds and shifts in temperature around you, there is an unlimited amount of material you can use in your own creative work.

Sometimes, imagining the connection between random objects can give you a fresh direction for a poem, story or essay.

Try this: Look around you, right now. Choose three objects that seem totally unrelated. Put them on a table near you. Start writing and find a way to incorporate each of the items as you go. *Challenge:* Mood is a vital element in writing. Let the objects help you discover a mood or feeling that shapes your work.

Tactile objects are powerful writing tools because you can use all of your senses to describe what is in your hand or right in front of you. What you hear can also evoke vivid writing. Take your journal to a coffee shop or museum. Find a chair or bench where you could sit for a while and listen to the pieces of conversation floating past you. Freely jot down words or phrases without editing or paying much attention to their meaning. After you have a collection of raw material, write a short essay or story using some or all of the material you overheard. *Challenge:* Write a scene, using overheard conversations. Make each character's voice distinctive and unique.

Writing
Experiment

rewrite
REWRITE
rewrite
until your
writing
sounds ~~write~~
right!

Chelsey Monroe, mentor

I wrote this at the Fiction Workshop, based on an experiment where different objects were taken out of bags and we had to insert them into our stories. I used the masquerade mask, wilted flower, rain boot, and football.

The Phantom Story

He was wearing it. *He* was wearing the mask. I cringed. Life couldn't get any worse. The ballroom spun brightly, colors colliding from the disco chandeliers against papier-mâché walls. Couples of all shapes circled the tiny dance floor, swaying to the sappy pop music like lilies in the wind. In *his* sweaty palms dangled wilted red roses, half-broken and barely clinging to harsh thorns. I tried not to cry. All my hopes – my romantic daydreams of a Parisian prince or a football champion were crushed under the heel of *his* cheap loafers. God, he acted like such a grandpa. I could almost imagine his hair receding before my eyes and his skin starting to crack.

Bethany, across the floor, peeked out at me through a delicate fan, her lenses changing color – red, blue, green, as the lights flashed by. It made me dizzy. I felt like I was going to faint, though whether it was because of my not-so-charming prince, or the room was open to question. I suddenly felt like I was trapped in a rainstorm as the clouds thundered above. All the color and feeling from my body drained slowly off me and down onto the wet pavement and into the nearest sewer. I was defeated. A single tear floated down my cheek as my body floated to the floor.

When I opened my eyes again, I was lying on crinkly paper with fluorescent lights above me, blinding. I moved slightly and the school nurse's head came into view.

"Strobe lights too much, huh? There's always a few of ya who can't handle it. You feeling better?"

I realized that I really had fainted on the dance floor. I turned my head toward the wall, hoping I could crawl inside myself until the night was over.

I Am a Metaphor

1. Metaphors can enhance your descriptions of people, places or things. Be a rubber band – stretch yourself to find at least 5 fresh ways to describe each of these very straightforward statements:

2. Pick an animal – any animal. Think about all the physical and sensory qualities of this animal. What does it see? How does it feel? Go beyond the cliche qualities of the animal. Discover the complex ways that you might describe yourself through identification with this creature.

- **I am cold.**
  (Examples: "I am a popsicle." "My feet are blocks of ice.")

- **She is determined.**
  ("She could climb a mountain.")

- **I love you.**
  ("You're the top. You're the Eiffel Tower." "You are my rock.")

- **The clouds were white and fluffy.**
  ("The clouds were spun cotton.")

- **I had a busy day.**
  ("Today was a tornado.")

Writing
Experiment

You know you're a writer when you stay up until

3:00 am

writing a book.

Myra Hollis, age 18

Butterfly

Free.
Joyful.
Delicate.

I am
a butterfly
coasting through life.

I can make it
through anything
no matter how hard it may seem.

I am
a butterfly.

Writing is Moving

1. Watch someone performing a task. Examine their motions – does it remind you of anything? What are all the ways you could describe their activity, without literally saying what they are doing? What emotions might be hidden behind their movements? Make a list of your observations. Then write a poem using phrases from your list. Mix up the order of the lines. Close your poem with an image or idea that summarizes what you observed.

2. In building a vivid character, it can be powerful to describe how the character moves, specifically. Does she slam down her pen on her desk or does she place it delicately, letting her fingers slowly let go? Does she brush her hair briskly or gently comb through every lock? Does she throw on a sweatshirt, or carefully slide her arms into a fine wool cardigan? Choose a character that you have already created (or create a new one!) and fully describe a few of their everyday movements, allowing us to more fully see who they really are.

Lizette Vargas, age 15

This piece was inspired by the Poetry Workshop, where we had to guess what our partner was doing with their hands, except they couldn't talk. It was very fun!

A Beautiful Silhouette

She neatly folded the paper,
Making sure all the folds were precise
Her hands moved happily, swiftly
Straightening, twisting, turning, pressing,
Her creativity had taken over,
And so she would sit,
Dedicatedly
Working on the corner of the table,
And now all that's left
Is her beautiful silhouette

Be curious about everything in the world.

Word Stacks

Can a grocery list be poetry? Or a to-do list? How about your Christmas list?

Absolutely they can, but probably not without a bit of tinkering. "Eggs, bread, milk, cat food" is not much of a poem, but add a little detail – "eggs for devilling, that thick black bread I ate in Minsk" – and you're on your way.

A list poem is just that – a list of things, any things, the more detailed the better. Try one of these:

- Things that make you smile

- Things that are old

- Things that are scary

- Things you see/pass on the way to school

- I wish…

- Home is where…

- Things that bug you

- Thing to do when you can't sleep

- Things that are square

- Things that are red

- My other self is…

- Everything you ate in the last week

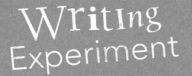

Writing
Experiment

Jillian Davis, age 18

I wrote this at the WriteGirl Poetry Workshop at the list poetry station.

Things That Are Red

Chinese New Year that turns a new page and opens a new envelope
Exit signs that light the way in a crisis
Strawberries, which actually have more vitamin C than oranges
My favorite color, because it can go with anything
Jack's hair, even though it's really not that red –
not ginger red, Jack red
Blood, which keeps me alive, breathing, and reluctantly blushing
My homecoming dress, back when I had essays to write
and someone to love
My emergency mini flashlight
Part of that ugly scarf I got in St. Malo
Boston University
My camera that has been replaced through museum drops
and the unforgiving sand of France
The carpet I will someday walk on
My eyes, after studying, writing, and thinking in French all night
Time in my room, which I rely on more than my appendix
Red Delicious apples, because they taste like a crispy summer,
which needs
to be here
ASAP

Write your
feelings.
Feel your
writing.

Mash-up

Sometimes, writing can be like cooking—you have to work with the ingredients you have on hand. Open your journal to a random page and choose any line that jumps out at you— write it down on a fresh page. Now flip ahead a few pages and find another phrase to add. Keep going until you fill a page. Now look it all over, and see how you can rearrange, rewrite and cut/ paste to create an entirely new piece of writing. *Variation:* Cut out each line with scissors, and rearrange them onto a new page. Use a bit of tape or glue to hold it all together.

Lauren Heaney, age 15

I wrote this during the Poetry Workshop at WriteGirl. Originally, it was four separate poems, each extremely short, so for the anthology, I combined words and lines from them to make a new poem.

Rage

The rage rolled in
Like a desire you can't decipher
Above the darkness alone
Its brilliant downward spiral of emotion
Jealous of
A cloudless sky

Walking from the garden
A path it makes on its own
With blankness fallen from
A paradise overlooked
Building the effect and size
Of rage

It's ok to go outside
the
box

because poetry can take
you to places you have never
been before.

Sticky Notes

Think about someone close to you. Write something specific that you admire about them on a sticky note, and place it on any blank surface – it could be a wall, a table, a door, the bathroom mirror or a large platter. Using free association, allow that first word to inspire a new word or phrase on another sticky note. Keep writing until your surface is filled with notes.

Take a week to grow your word collage even more – add new notes, but resist the temptation to take anything away. Sometimes inspiration takes time, and stories need to unfold. At the end of the week, look at all of your notes, and find the one note that will begin your story or poem, then choose at least one other note that you will incorporate into your writing.

Jamai Fisher, age 16

Short and sweet and to the point, my "mentor for the day" and I used sticky notes to create a collage of beautifulness!

Air

The penetrating blue sky
  Was discontent
Melodic dark breezes
  Rolled in like a jealous
Rage of mutiny against
    Perfect air.

write in different surroundings.

mix it

Don't stay in the same → location

UP

Flash Fiction

A story doesn't have to be an epic tale. You can tell a whole story in six words, in five sentences or in one minute. Create your own rules to strictly limit the length of your story, then start writing, keeping in mind some of the key elements of great fiction: characters are more interesting when they transform or change, stories are more powerful when there is tension or suspense, endings are gripping when they have an unexpected twist and beginnings are inviting when they start in the middle of the scene. And remember – one very specific detail can tell volumes about a character or place.

In the following examples of flash fiction, you can see how Lisa and Gabriella have created entire worlds and vivid characters with a few well-chosen words. *Your turn! Go!*

Writing
Experiment

Gabriella Evans, age 18

In our one-on-one mentoring sessions, we've been writing flash fiction inspired by a random word generator. For these stories, we used the word "wig" and limited ourselves to thirty words.

No More Dress Up

The boy's chubby fingers slid out from underneath the rim perfectly
So the long blonde wig almost looked natural.
He smiled at himself in the mirror
Until the door opened.

Lisa Beebe, mentor

Backstage

Beneath the glossy wig, false lashes, heavy eyeliner, and shimmery shadow, she saw her own eyes in the mirror. She turned away – fast – from the judgmental stare. Showtime.

Gabriella Evans, age 18

We used the word "tears" and challenged ourselves to write stories that were five sentences or fewer.

Spiderweb

Her tears hit the paper, smearing the ink
Creating what looked like fibers of a spiderweb.
She gripped the pen harder as her withered old hand began to shake.
Her cracking acrylic nails reminded her of the life she once lived
Before death caught up.
Her pen made one final loop at the bottom of the note
Before it hit her dirty hospital gown
And the monitor stopped its quiet beeping
And became one loud screech.

Lisa Beebe, mentor

Unfair

She sipped her lemonade, trying not to cry.

Who breaks up with someone – someone they've been dating three months – in the Tunnel of Love ride? He must care more about having a funny breakup story to tell his friends than he'd ever cared about her. Tears, tears, tears.

She took a deep breath, sipped another sip, and realized she liked the way lemonade tastes through a tear-salted straw more than she'd ever liked him.

it will
be
epic

Kristen Lee, age 16

I wrote this piece after reading some poems in the WriteGirl anthology, "Intensity," that took an object or image and gave it a new story. I was also inspired by the book, "The Catcher in the Rye," and past experiences when my longtime friends chose to spend more time with other people.

Ham Sandwich

I knew you before she did,
Back when your legs were twigs
Ambling the wrong direction
In the crowded hallways,
Back when your hair was a mousy brown mop,
Back when a string of ants on the sidewalk
Could captivate you for four hours.
We shared a rubbery ham sandwich
That my mom packed for me that one Tuesday
When the bullies stole your lunch,
And I smiled, despite their teasing,
As we shared our halves of the sandwich.

Now, I watch you pass by me every day
As you stroke your perfectly coiffed hair,
Flipped over to one side.
You march on the sidewalk,
Wearing shiny black designer sneakers
With your arm around that girl –
You've probably stomped about
One hundred ants in the process.
All I can do is stare; I try to eat,
I grab a ham sandwich out of my backpack,
But my stomach aches; I throw it away,
Knowing I'll never have my other half again.

write like a sculptor
who creates her own
marble — pour out your
words without judgement.
you can chip away at
them later.

Zoe Isabella Camp, age 17

First Year

Two people. A boy and a girl. Very much alike in personality, but very different in a sense. A story so tragic. So unique. So romantic. So painful, it's almost impossible to describe. An age difference that tears the two apart. An ex-love that keeps returning. A battle for love, friendship, security, trust, and that one friend who ended up in the middle of it all. Welcome to my freshman year of high school.

Guadalupe Mendoza, age 15

While writing together at Starbucks, my mentor and I found an article online about the most overused words from 2011 and decided to use them all. Here are the words we had to incorporate into our writing: viral, epic, refudiate, literally, bro, hater, hating, totes, amazing, and "Google" used as a verb.

2011 Lingo Bashing

She's such a hater, bro.

She doesn't understand my epicness.

Literally, bro.

I'm like, amazing.

Just look at me!

When my workout vids go viral,

It will be epic.

Totes.

She's just hating on me, like me? Bro, me? Come on.

She needs a reality check. She can't refudiate these abs…

Google it.

you

are

the creator of
this universe
of your writing.

Use that wisely.

Astghik Hairapetian, age 17

Despite campaigns that vouch for the beauty of all body types, it's hard not to notice that there is still an ideal for beauty. This poem is made of snippets from an issue of Teen Vogue.

Teen Vogue Found Poem

Beauty that
Removes easily with nail polish
just might damage your health

What happens when
A six-foot-five plus size girl
takes direction from an unlikely source?
GUESS

Brazilian-born bombshells,
younger plus-size women,
the deadly but popular combo
It was a fairytale moment, for sure

I can't be myself

No More Guessing
The verdict is unanimous:
beauty
has become nothing short of the holy grail

Join the millions of women who have found their
True Religion

Stefanie Michelle Almendárez, mentor

I wrote this piece last year, inspired by a prompt from the poet Dorianne Laux.

scaffolding

"Desiderata" on cold sunny mornings meant that Mom appreciated God, her life and her kids. El Grupo Niche put Mom in the mopping mood. Simon & Garfunkel unraveled Dad as he sipped his Corona, the *L.A. Times* in his hands.

On a dawn of clacking ladders, the stench of tar woke us up, and Dad with his glasses scribbled hurried writing and geometry – brown stains from his unstable coffee while driving colored his black and white composition notebook. A Perfect Circle's song, *3 Libras*, a red star lamp purchased at CityWalk set the mood for my sister's bittersweet thoughts over her doomed relationships.

Tony Hawk's pro skater game was my little brother's soundtrack. At barely ten, he drummed along with Union 13 and System Of A Down – his favorite bands. He'd skateboard, as Mom encouraged him to; he wanted to lose weight for the girls in his class who loved his spiked hair, his green eyes, and smarty-pants.

My sweet little stereo enclosed my own concert: Blink 182's *Take Off Your Pants and Jacket* and my bootleg CD of 80s flashbacks. Behind white wooden walls, I remember glow-in-the-dark stars. At night, I'd dream I was camping – fantasizing with my first boyfriend ever, writing love poems, writing since I was ten, diary after diary, no longer collecting Hello Kitty, Winnie the Pooh on white sheets, cucumber melon cream on just-shaved legs, Lip Smacker's chapstick on unkissed lips, hearts open wide for Father, Mother, Sister, Brother, and I would surely soon see the rain…

Shelby Campbell, age 14

I wrote this poem when one of my friendships wasn't going as planned.
I wondered how they would react if I were to run away.

I Wonder

If I ran away, would you care? Would you cry or worry?
Would it hurt?
Would things be different?
Would you constantly wonder, or be afraid?
Or would you care less?

Would you be able to focus?
Would you fail?
Would you mourn?
Or would everything stay the same?

Would you come after me? Would you search high and low?
Would you not give up until I'm found?
Would you save me?

If I ran away, would you change?

Majah Carberry, age 17

I wrote this piece during a session with my mentor, Retta. We were working on poetry and decided to write a piece about sleep. I changed it slightly, and made it a piece about being stuck in dreams.

Sleep

Deeper within, shapes here are unstable,
Dizzy, and clouded, my hand wavers
In five colors.
I try to use unsteady magic
To pull my heavy body
Out from the dense, sinking sea.
Shapes here are clearer, but
Words are thrown off, striking
Strangely in my ears.
Sticky sap, stick fast, as
I am all too wakeful within this sleep.
Movement without moving, in a panic
I cannot tell if I am rising
Or falling.
But I would never fall or die
So then I must surface.
Blankets cover sense and guilt
Fires hot and senseless
Within my belly, but
I am too tired, and the world
Isn't ready to face my fears just yet.
I fall again, or rise.
Then sink.

Retta Putignano King, mentor

I wrote this during a session with my mentee, Majah. We wrote from a prompt about being under water. When we shared our work afterwards, it was interesting to see that we had both used similar words, giving the pieces the same feel and texture.

Abyss

Open my eyes
To the murky depths
Wisps of hair
Float past my face
Free
Mocking me
The quiet unnerves my core
Flashes of light
Piercing
Dancing
Begging me to play
And yet I sink
The deep opens its arms
And holds me strong
I forget to breathe
There is no need

write through the chaos.
If you're stuck, write
through the stuck.

Brianna Solorio, age 14

The Many Faces of Love

She always saw him as one of the sweetest boys in school, until he showed his true colors. It seemed as if his heart were a black hole, filled to the brim with ice. How can someone treat another human being like a piece of gum stuck to the end of a shoe?

She admired the way he always seemed to acknowledge her in one way or another, making her feel as if she was finally important. But there were many hurtful encounters to come.

She was hurt and confused. Should she cry?! No! She could not show this side of her. She would not let him see her like that. He does not love me! She repeated these words in her head countless times. He said it himself. But why? What had she done wrong?

She played back the times they had spent together. Nothing came to her. "Maybe," she thought, "maybe I was being too needy? Maybe I was not giving him enough attention." Yes, that was it. She could fix this mess, she thought to herself. If I give him all of my attention and all of my unconditional love, he will love me again! She picked up the phone and dialed his number.

Love can be kind and it can be sweet. It can also have a side as dark as the color of a black leather jacket. Poor girl. Why would anyone put up with that?

Sara Kimura, age 17

Looking back on a busy month and thinking about the many tasks still before me, I wondered where all my time had gone. I always lose things, so it was fun to treat time as an object that I can, and do, actually misplace.

Last Thursday

I've misplaced my time
somewhere between now –
and last Thursday.
It can't be far though –
I was holding it not twenty minutes ago,
it seems.
Let's retrace the seconds –
perhaps I dropped a few
on my way out the door.
Think real hard now –
When was the last time I had it?
Perhaps when I did the dishes,
it slipped right down the drain.
Or perhaps I could have deleted it,
when I forgot to save my Melville essay…

When's the last time I saw it?
It was Thursday, I suppose,
I had my time –
And then life dropped by,
And that's all I'll ever know.

Use punctuation, in unexpected places, to add depth, to your writing.

Zzzzah-Zzaz Burnley, age 16

A boy I really liked inspired me to write this piece.

Uncertainty

I'm Zzzzah-Zzaz.
Confused. Around you,
I'm shy.

You've asked me out
not once,
But a thousand times.

I still haven't said yes.

"Do you want to go out with me?"
"No."
"When you figure it out, let me know."

You ask me again.

I respond: "It's complicated."
"Why?"
"There's something in the way."

You pout,
I shout. You walk,
I stay.

I stand here
on display. A very
confused person.

Anna Henry, mentor

During the Fiction Workshop, we talked about writing using details from sensory observation. This is loosely based on a memory from my teens.

Popular

You were tall, had long straight red hair, and were the best student in the class – the one picked to be the captain of the soccer team. You were a natural at everything, and I wanted to be in your aura. You'd talk to me after school because you thought I was "interesting," and I'd walk you home to the big, modern, sparkling, empty house where your dad was never home.

I wanted to be special, whatever that meant – to be recognized and thought of and mentioned by you. Sometimes, but rarely, it happened. You invited me for a Saturday – a whole day on a weekend, not after school – at your weekend house. Just you and me, finally, though I didn't know what we'd do with a whole Saturday by ourselves.

I took the train out. I walked along the gravel to the street. I found the house with the pressed linen curtains and the weeping willow outside. There were voices and giggling, a sort of happy shriek, a dog barking, dishes clanking, a game going on. At the doorstep, I could see five, maybe six girls, the ones you'd sit with at lunch, the ones who were like you. I turned around and took the next train home.

Pull experiences from your
life and put them into
your writing. It makes
it all the more awesome.

Rachel Burdorf, age 15

*Every once in a while, stop and take a deep breath and find
the peace around you.*

Days of Summer

The sun is a molten blob of metal
submerged in the aquamarine sky.

I half expect it to boil and steam
and evaporate into space.

It is a contrast
too extreme to last until sunset.

Sooner or later
the scale has to tip.

    It always does.

But in the meantime
I kick off my cleats.

And let the sun warm my toes.
They're painted purple today.

I'm alright.
I'm alright.

electric

current

write down your
dreams - If you can't
remember your dreams
when you wake up,

make one up.

Sara Lenski, age 16

This is an excerpt from a novel that I have been working on. I started writing it when I was going through a difficult time in my life and I saw how many people were there for me.

The Rain

A raindrop fell on my forehead. As I was sitting up to stand, I wrinkled my nose. Alex pulled me to his side as we sat in the grass.

"Hate the rain," I muttered.

"There's no harm in getting a little wet."

"Hate the rain," I repeated. Alex sighed, standing up. I looked up at him and he stared back, waiting for me to get up. I put both my hands up, asking him silently to help me to my feet. He rolled his eyes playfully, muttered something that sounded like "lazy" under his breath, grabbed my hands, and helped me to my feet. But, he pulled me to him and I ended back up in his embrace. Not that I really minded, but, oh well. Alex took my left hand in his right and put his left on my lower back.

"Will you dance?" he asked me.

I bit my lip. "You know I hate to."

"There is no one around to see you and it's raining. You really can't get more romantic than this."

"Never knew you were such a romantic," I said quietly. I sighed in defeat, and put my hand on Alex's shoulder. As we moved in a small circle, I thought about how much I loved him, even though he embarrassed me. After all, we were dancing in the rain.

Isabella Lloyd-Damnjanovic, age 16

This was written for my boyfriend, who helped me get through a difficult period last summer.

Awake Again

My hours were measured in stray eyelashes,
blowing dandelions,
waiting and what if-ing, starving on empty hope.
I was drowning in oxygen with nowhere to surface
that first time I touched you.
You were so real, palpable.
You were cool blades of grass under ash grey, squirrely trees,
sunset on the metro station.
You were an untie-able tie, running past the freeway,
jumping in elevators.
You were a spark on the lucky gong, a too-salty kumquat,
the beginning of time in a warm dark theater,
dancing to Satie in a box of tingles.
You were a head on my shoulder,
an arm around my waist, fingers intertwined –
propane and hexane and 2,3-isopropylyourmom!,
free donuts and splintered chopsticks.
You were sweeping golden lashes and kisses on my nose,
an electric current, and "ha," "ma."
Endless and infinite.
You were so real, tangible.
Confidently waiting, swimming in light and full of tomorrows,
exponentially green.
I touched you, and that sluggish beat, it woke again
and in an instant,
the sky was bluer than it'd ever been.

Marielle Bagnard, age 16

This piece is a short moment in a dramatic "breakup scene." I was inspired to show how we find ourselves in battle with ourselves.

The Breakup

"I'm sick and tired of being told I don't care – or try enough! I wasn't sure how I felt before, but now I know – I don't have feelings for you anymore. Are you happy now?!"

As soon as he said it, he knew he didn't mean it. For the first time, there was complete silence. He towered in the heat of the moment, ready to lash out again at whatever she had to say. He let out an exasperated breath, redness still glued to his face, hands clenched in tight fists.

Her body wilted. Tears began to flow down her cheeks. All she did was to say one word: "Yes."

He crumbled. His organs sank to the floor and he wished (more than anything) to take it all back, but his heart was the furthest from him. His eyes widened as hers weakened. A guilty blush washed over his face, and the color left her skin.

She let all of his daggers hit her at once. Unable to move, her eyes on the floor, she croaked, "See you around."

As she turned her back on him, his tongue felt a shock, and from deep in his throat he managed to cry out, "Maggie…"

– but nothing more.

Christina Guillen, mentor

I was given the prompt "What if?" and I thought, "What if life were literally black-and-white, like an old photo?"

Tango Blanco y Negro

What if my world were black-and-white, not in a depressing way, but in an SLR camera in a café in Argentina kinda way? I can hear violins where he lifts me up and cello where he drops me down. The patrons sitting at tables for two pause instead of sipping their whisky and small clinking ice. All eyes are on us as we tell a story of passion and sadness that is love with the dance we do in dim lighting. My black-toed heels dragging the tiled floor where he has swept me so low. Where I can't see color, I hear music, I feel textures. My world is black-and-white, but my senses are on fire. A woman leaves a stain of lipstick on her man, not her glass.

Getting stuck in your writing isn't the end, it's only a PAUSE to make it better.

Dilcia Aviles, age 18

In Her Slumber

The woman and man sat close to each other under the night sky. They searched for the moon in the sea of stars. They sat together in silence, observing the constellations, and at times, drowned in each other's eyes. The woman smiled.

When she sought his gaze, wondrous thoughts filled her mind, and when those thoughts lingered, she could do nothing more than allow her cheeks to flush in a bright pink. The man hummed. He sang to the woman he loved a lullaby and held her closely against the build of his chest. Their hearts thumped simultaneously, synchronizing to the night's love. He rocked, cradling the woman, and let her fall sound asleep to his song. The man entwined his fingers with hers and smiled. He whispered in her ear, wishing her sweet dreams.

Her translucent skin sparkled in the night sky, shimmering as if encased by diamonds. She giggled and reached for him. Her hands, with long, soft fingers, cupped his face, their mouths just a few inches away. His lips curved up to a grin – so beautiful that she could not hold back. Their lips met, which held them close to the dream world.

The stars danced along, rearranging themselves as the horizon welcomed the breaking of dawn. He shook his head and stared at the rise of the Morning Star. She sighed, struggling to be by his side. The only moment the woman and the spirit of her dead love could embrace was in the dream world, as she lay asleep. Both knew this and were left with pain. But morning rose now, and her body shifted. Unwillingly, she awoke; her eyes lazily fluttered open. She gazed at the sun and sighed once more.

Lost in memory, she thought about the romantic clouds that curtained her heart. Tonight will be another dream, she reflected, and rose for the adventure of today.

Patti Hawn, mentor

This is an excerpt from a blog piece I wrote about all the things we do for our girlfriends.

Stuff we do for girlfriends…

It occurred to me as I was rushing this morning at 7 a.m. to my BFF's house, to provide emotional support for her during a heated financial "discussion" with her ex-husband, all the things we just "do" when asked. We cancel appointments; take time off of work; slip into small, mirrored, badly-lit dressing rooms to give honest critiques; loan our best clothes; tell the truth – no matter what.

When called upon, we "just do it," even when we don't want to, because that's just what women do for women. We tread where others do not dare. We become warriors for each other – warning others "not to go there." We share yucky secrets (the ones we can barely put into words), like that humiliating date we'd rather forget.

We learn to recognize the small shifts in each other's voices that tell us it's time for a lunch or a long phone conversation, even if it's the same conversation we've been having for years. We simply listen – and we never, ever bring it up again, no matter what. We tell each other the hard stuff and we love each other fiercely, instinctively… and often longer than our marriages. Long live girlfriends!

Write down everything!
You'd be surprised what random
bursts of inspiration can lead you to.

Amayian 'Melisa' Arauz, age 17

The Words I Can't Say

Not one minute goes by that I'm not reminded of you. Sometimes I forget that things between us ended and I get the urge to text or call you, but I always stop myself. I can't go to the theaters without remembering you. There was that time we saw *Real Steel* and I spilled Starbucks in my purse, or the time we saw *Jack and Jill* and I broke one of the buttons on your shirt. We couldn't stop laughing.

Everything I do reminds me of you. I still love you. Sometimes I try to hate you just so I can feel angry. I try to remember the things that drove me crazy about you, the things that made me mad, but then I realize these are some of the same reasons why I love you.

I'll never forget the way you laughed or your usual order at Starbucks (venti vanilla bean). I'll never forget your beautiful eyes, strong arms, and intoxicating scent of fresh laundry and Old Spice. I miss staring into your eyes and being able to see all the stars in the galaxy, but most of all, I miss your lips and the way one kiss was all it took to brighten up my day. I miss the things that made us *us*. I miss you.

I've never felt so vulnerable in my life. It pains me to think that what we had meant nothing to you, but you showed me that I could love someone with all my heart. You showed me what is beautiful about being in love. So for that, thank you.

Love you always,
Meli

S

11 Challenges

The
stars
tell my
secrets

Daniella Faura, age 13

I was inspired to write this piece after listening to Elton John's song "Rocket Man." I thought to myself, "How would I feel up in space?"

What Spacemen Must Feel

I curse and crave this distance
And having only the stars to tell my secrets.
Even though they're light-years away,
They somehow find a way to listen.
The unhurried orbit makes me nostalgic
For what used to be before the voyage.
I've been up here so many times before
And it's starting to show.
When the engine burns low
And when I do descend,
I buff my goggles to see
That living amongst the Roman planets
And twinkling stars, gets lonely.

write to be
speechless.

Gina Corso, mentor

I was grieving over the death of a friend – pain is a strong source of writing motivation for me.

Hallelujah

Eight o'clock sharp, I pulled up in front of her parents' home. In the gloaming, all that was visible were the silhouettes of fellow mourners. My feet shuffled down the hall of their home. I drowned in the thickness of pungent flower bouquets and oceanic tears. "You look so well, my dear, so good to see you," the father sputtered, "We have always kept our eye on you, and it has been such a relief to see that you are well again, dear." He embraced me, and I felt a peculiar connection with this wilting patriarch.

As the week passed, I found myself wondering what hid around each corner. I pored over books of anatomy. Learned the difference between the aorta, and the pulmonary artery. One takes care of the lungs. Oxygen-deficient blood flows through the vena cava. Rinse. Repeat. Passing waves of electrical impulses signal life or death.

I simultaneously cursed my slipping transmission and God as I shifted gears, driving to the church for the funeral – the same church that witnessed me whisper my first confession. Its walls remembered. It smelled like fly dust and stale flowers. The pews were lined up in slim rows before me, and slender black ghosts filed in, one by one. I sat before the marble Jesus. The dark eyes of Jessica stared back at me from her portrait on the altar; her dark hair was long in this picture, but not long enough to reach home. I felt myself slipping into my past. Thoughts raced wildly alongside all the times I threw my life about so recklessly, like a deck of cards up in the air. Hustling my own death. Old memories lashed me like a fierce whip cracking against my bare skin.

Iyana Banks, age 16

Waves

Waves crash over me
Back and forth
Pulling me this way and that
Like a game of tug-o'-war

The challenge is not escaping –
It is to choose a direction
But how can you,
If neither choice is right?

Think fast
Though the choice is hard,
I know I can help myself.

Yenis Coto, age 14

Sometimes

Sometimes
the people closest to you
end up hurting you.
and the people farthest from you
end up helping you.

What happens
when love wants nobody,
and pain wants everybody?

You are ice, I am fire.

The people you never thought of
will end up loving you the most,
will help you cure the pain you've been through.

A terrifying storm can become a vivid rainbow.

Lauren Archer, mentor

This piece was written during an in-schools session at Azusa. We each pulled a card with a random topic and had to write about it, but also be specific.

Things That Bug Me

Slow drivers in the fast lane.
People who chew with their mouths open.
Falling in because my brother left the toilet seat up...again.
A discourteous teen constantly kicking the back of my seat
at a late-night movie.
That annoying sales lady at Macy's or Nordstrom
who follows you around to make sure you're not stealing...
as if there aren't cameras in the store.
Ordering a burger with no tomatoes at a drive-thru,
leaving the window, then checking my order only to realize
there are tomatoes on my burger.
People who constantly come up to my daughter and me,
only to ask dumb questions:
"What are you mixed with?"
"Did you dye your daughter's hair?"
"Is her father white?"
"Is your father white?"
Why are you asking me?

Janel Pineda, age 15

I feel as though depression and suicide are not always taken seriously in our society. The things that bring us the most happiness often bring us the most suffering.

Bittersweet Melancholy of Nostalgia, an excerpt

As the world around her began to fall apart, she picked up the pieces and tucked them away safely in the pockets of her jeans and beneath empty floorboards and onto the highest shelf of the cabinet and into every crevice that she could manage to find.

She stored them between the pages of her favorite books and in the simple breath that a musician takes before beginning to play the last song of the evening. She slipped them into her morning coffee and sewed them into the folds of her skirts.

Every now and then, she stumbles across her room and finds bits of others and bits of herself. These fragments have manifested themselves into the petals of flowers and into the laces in her boots and even in the dash of cinnamon in her dessert. What with their jaggedness, they punctured the tires of her car, not unlike the way that they have also wounded her heart. As she tosses and turns in her sleep, she finds that it was not a pea beneath her mattress that had served as a disruption, but rather, one of these pieces.

She turns the debris over in the palms of her hands, brushing past them ever so carefully with the tips of her fingers. These mangled shards have brought her a great deal of suffering, but somehow simultaneously have made her the happiest that she has ever been.

YOUR LIFE IS THE BEST MATERIAL
FOR A STORY. LOVE YOURSELF AND
YOUR
VOICE.

Kathleen DiPerna, mentor

Night

There's a riot in the street.
Lock all the doors. Turn off the lights.
Don't come for her. She's done for tonight.
Sometimes it's best to let it go up in flames.

Everything's lost, she whispered.
Only ash and brokenness remain.
A thousand shards of glass catch one glint of sun.
Sometimes the best of things are meant to come undone.

With everything she's lost tonight,
With all this empty aching space,
Something new buds inside her,
Something new you'll never take.

She is stronger than this night.
She is stronger than this night.
She is stronger than this night.

Edna Cerritos, age 16

This is a combination of two poems I wrote during a mentoring session.

Who I Am

I am a believer.
Within myself,
a color that's undefined.

I am a color that changes daily.
I believe miracles happen
daily.

I am a believer. A survivor.
I change and grow
like you.

I am a color that is everywhere,
a survivor of a journey.
A journey that is…
unbelievable.

We're Having

CAKe tOnight

Find your hour.
Write when you feel most inspired and if that doesn't work, eat chocolate and then start writing again.

Cree Nixon, age 18

Having a crush as a teenage girl is super sweet. I wanted to write a poem about how I felt and how I experienced him like one would experience the perfectly blended mint tea.

Like Honey

Your words
like honey.
Your accent
like sipping mint tea.
Our conversation
like rich coffee
perfectly seasoned with our own
special blend of cinnamon and sugar.
When I suck this cup of Joe dry,
maybe next year I'll prefer
an iced mocha kind of guy.

Lyna Moreno, age 14

My mom recently changed our lifestyle, especially in the food department.

Super Health Freak

I don't like how everything's changed in the fridge. When I pull out the jelly, it says 15% more fruit. Don't get me wrong, I love strawberry jelly, but just the jelly part. I don't want half-cut strawberries lodged in my jelly. Where did all this health junk and peaceful living come from?

A book of inspirational quotes stands on the counter in the kitchen. All our bread is whole wheat. Other food and beverages are labeled "reduced fat" or "lighter." I see less and less soda. This does not excite me in any way. Did I mention having to take gummy bear vitamins?

Healthy is good, but I'm not all ears for it. Cheesy posters and cartoons about the food pyramid just don't fit my eating style. Whatever my mom is doing isn't working. I won't give up my junk food that easily.

I never think of vegetables the way I think about chips. My favorite food: bagels. Now, even the cream cheese is low in fat. It feels like she's been baby-proofing the food.

It's Thursday, so my mom goes off to aerobics class. That seems pointless to me. I'm not sure losing 50 calories is a big accomplishment.

When she leaves, I eat all the things she never buys for us anymore. Fries, donuts, and high-in-fat pizza. I try to think of what I can do to defy her healthiness, to destroy any peace living in this household. I play rock music. Panic! At the Disco, which isn't heavy metal but it will do.

WRITE SOMETHING EVERY DAY

Anne Ramallo, mentor

I wrote this piece during a WriteGirl In-Schools Workshop in which we practiced using sensory language to describe food.

Waffles

My Grandma Joyce is like Willy Wonka – always with the right sweet treat for any situation. Upset stomach? Vanilla ice cream is good for digestion. When I was playing in the park and a bitter, soapy bubble landed in my mouth it was, "Let's go home and get some jelly beans." And every morning when I woke up in her big spare bed, the hum of Ham Lane outside the window and the smell of lavender always faintly perceptible, I could look forward to waffles with strawberries and whipped cream.

My grandma had a year-round supply of strawberries in her freezer. All she had to do was defrost and there was a bowl of squishy, sweet strawberries. Their syrupy juice would soak through the waffles, turning them into a soggy pile of bread that melted between your tongue and the roof of your mouth. And then the whipped cream! Not just white foam from a can or bucket, but something that was alive in a cow last week. She would pour fresh cream into a bowl and beat it with her hand mixer until the liquid stood up in confident peaks. An oversized tablespoon dollop would fall onto the waffle with such a satisfying, dull thud.

These small indulgences, in the comfort of Grandma Joyce's plush, upholstered barstools taught me how entirely possible it is to create my own beautiful, delicious world. No matter what a day holds, a plate of juicy waffles can get things off to a good start and a handful of jelly beans in the afternoon can overpower the bitterness of a long, dry work meeting. And for those times I'm literally sick with anxiety, there's always vanilla ice cream.

Zzzahkia Burnley, age 14

My mentor and I were eating at a café and she asked me to look around and write about what I saw and admired.

Pete's Café

Mid-city.
Downtown L.A.
Its architecture,
small buildings, big inspiration.

I am no longer color-blind –
green olives,
snow dogs outside,
fans, lights and lamps.

I feel I don't belong in these places.
I peek out the window,
look across the street.
A gypsy is dancing, she has no feet.

Refreshing…
Refreshing…
"Refreshments?"

"Oh, thank you."
"No, thank you! Please come again."

WRITE DURING BORING CLASS TIME. IT'LL MAKE THE CLASS FUN.

Annie Brown, mentor

During a workshop last year, I scribbled a few notes about a true experience. Those journal jottings prompted this fictionalized piece, which I wrote during a recent WriteGirl workshop.

Government Chicken

He opened the door and the fluorescent bulb popped on, lighting the clean white walls of the refrigerator. Except for the crusty mustard and ketchup bottles, it was empty. His stomach rumbled. He'd known there was nothing in there, but he had hope. Now his body sagged, defeated.

At the kitchen table, he leafed desperately through the *Yellow Pages* and dialed the number for government assistance. The next morning, he picked up two five-pound bags of corn grits, a wagon wheel of cheese, some assorted canned vegetables, and a huge bag of frozen chicken. He lugged the heavy bags up to his apartment and filled the cupboards. He sat down and his breath eased.

With no money for rent, he temporarily sublet his apartment and moved in with his girlfriend. He packed the chicken and brought it along.

Hoping to make himself useful, he looked up recipes, and bought groceries. As he defrosted the pink and yellow mass, he discovered that it was not three neat chickens, but an unappealing jumble of about thirty chicken thighs amid chunks of ice. It was going to be an all or nothing defrost situation.

He went for it. He stuffed chicken into pots boiling on the stove, and piled it into pans baking in the oven. He danced around the kitchen, pouring cream and spices into the pots, peeking in the oven from time to time. The smell of curry and apples wafted through the air, lining up the neighborhood cats outside the kitchen door.

Sasha Villarreal, age 14

I was inspired by the school production of "Sweeney Todd."

Cake House

"Okay," Jason whispered, "once we turn this corner, you can't back out of the dare. Go up to the house, knock, and enter." Once the teenagers turned the corner, Sean saw the house. As he approached, smoke escaped the chimney and the shingles on the rooftop clattered rapidly. The rocking chair swayed back and forth. Sean pushed the doorbell and everything stopped.

Slowly, the door creaked open and there stood the old lady. "Hello," she said.

Sean scratched the back of his head, "Um, is your house really haunted?"

The old lady sighed sadly, "Why don't you come in and I'll tell you my story?" Once the door closed, the old lady shuffled her way to the kitchen and came back with tea for Sean. "Now," she said, "the reason why everyone says that my house is haunted is because my mother murdered my friends."

Sean almost spit up his tea, "What?!"

"One day, I asked my mother to help me cook for the bake sale. She said she would, but I needed to bring my friends. I did. Then I was told to go to the store for some icing. When I came back, my friends were already a cake! There was blood everywhere! I called the police. My mother was arrested and I was put into a crazy house because they thought what I witnessed had made me hysterical."

"That's why everyone's afraid? Because your mother killed your friends?!"

"Well, maybe I killed one," the old lady said.

"What?" Sean asked, as he fell over dead.

Jason came out down from upstairs holding an ax, passing by the framed newspaper articles that read, "Insane Child Helps Mother Murder Her Friends" and "Child Escapes Mental Hospital."

"Good idea poisoning the tea," she said. "You're a good grandson. We're having cake tonight!"

Linda Folsom, mentor

This was done during a time when we were exploring different forms –
this poem is a pantoum.

Hunger

My stomach growls
Anxious to be fed
The refrigerator is bare
Leftovers are gone

Anxious to be fed
I consider other options
Leftovers are gone
Cheerios for dinner?

I consider other options
Mac & cheese perhaps
Cheerios for dinner?
I have no milk to pour

Mac & cheese perhaps
Requires only water
I have no milk to pour
Hallelujah, I have Top Ramen

Reparata Mazzola, mentor

I wrote this after my mentee and I were talking about family in one of our writing sessions.

Mamma Mia Mine

It was cold in Mrs. Arcati's basement beauty parlor. The chair was uncomfortable and I was scared.

"Make sure she doesn't look too Italian." The instruction was from my beautiful, Calabrese mother with the golden eyes and wavy black mane.

The old woman's pinking shears snipped around my head, thinning my thick, dark tresses. Then came the fire, singeing my bangs to straighten them. I looked like a Mediterranean scarecrow. What on earth was my mother doing? In retrospect, I know…she was protecting me.

Mama had lived through the war, when Italians were the enemy. Even though all the men in our family went overseas to fight for America (and miraculously all came back), that ghostly stigma remained.

Growing up in Brooklyn, I could not relate to that prejudice. My parents had jumped feet first into the melting pot. Dad was the first Sicilian-Catholic officer at a major bank. We had a house, a car and a good middle-class life. And despite trying to make me all-American, Mom maintained our Italian traditions, like lasagna as a first course at Thanksgiving and meatballs that have made me a legend in my circle.

Thanks, Mamma Mia Mine, for always having my back.

13 Music

majestic noises

Laura Lujan, age 16

This piece was written late at night when I couldn't handle any more homework.

I Just Discovered Jazz

Taken from the world surrounding,
Into piano affair
Whirling
Twirling
Tapping of feet
Happiness lingers
A sweet soft place
Saxophones, trumpets
Call me
Tenderly in the night
They call to me
Urge me
Black and white keys dancing
High
Low
Majestic noises blending
With the silence of the night
For a moment it's just me
Home

Vivian Tran, age 14

This song is for a friend who's confused about her crush.

Not a Stupid Love Song

Chorus:
This is not a stupid love song
Not like the ones you hear on the radio
I think you got it all wrong
Because I know it's not a stupid love song

Verse:
Since I saw you yesterday
I haven't been the same
I thought you were just a friend
Random moments made a change
These feelings I can't comprehend
I never thought it was true
But I can't stop thinking about you

Write bored.
Write angry.
Write terrible.
Just write.
Things will change.

Kamrin Mara, age 15

This piece was written late at night, inspired by a fantastical dream.

The Secret Song

The moon shone upon the hidden pond, enveloped by the surrounding woods. Lilies and toads silently slept, awaiting the arrival of the little girl. An enchanting mist slinked over the pond and subsided, temporarily revealing a young girl dressed in night robes. She always came to this pond, and always at the second hour after the moon had shown his face. Her presence awoke and attracted all the dormant animals of the day, who had become accustomed to her nightly stay.

The high-pitched crickets hopped in front of the low-toned toads as other pond creatures filed into their usual seats. Once in their places, the rows of insects and wildlife peered up at their human composer. The young girl smiled as her blue eyes reflected the enchanting scene unfolding before her. She drew in a deep breath as the orchestra of untamed musicians readied their instruments. The soothingly high tone of the young girl's voice carried through the woods into the village, planting smiles on the people in the sleeping town. Her innocent song was a bright star in the night, revealing nature's secrets.

Majah Carberry, age 17

I wrote this poem after listening to a beautiful song.

Sing

I once knew where to walk
And how to discern, those,
All of those words,
I sang it twice, in my head.
Sacred things, I tried to hear
When the whisper fell on the wind
But I couldn't, could not,
And I fell the hardest I ever had fallen.
Red, dancing red heart
Pulled on and on
While my blood sang the song
My voice couldn't match.
There's too much light to die,
Too many mountains to fall,
So one day, we'll walk on the beach,
And maybe yesterday or now, it will all work.

Piers Gunter, age 17

Left Home

Verse:
you said you were busy
you were out with a friend
but I don't believe you

you said you wrote a letter
and forgot to hit send
but I don't believe you

Chorus:
you're with her
I'm alone,
wake up to an empty home,
the doors are open,
the lights are on,
but you're away.
I never had the chance
to ask you to stay.

Jackelyne Cuellar, age 17

*This poem was inspired by the annoying "music" made by the
animals in my neighborhood.*

If I Could Talk To Animals

If I could talk to animals,
I'd tell my cockatiel, Casey
to shut her beak at 6 a.m. on Saturday morning.
I'd ask my other cockatiel, Lucky,
why he loves to eat my homework.

I'd ask the dog across my street
why he likes to bark at night and
if he is just simply scared of the dark.

Then I'd talk to the stray cats
that linger wild and free,
about how much fun it is
to be outdoors and why
they act like lions roaming my yard.

I'd ask them how it feels to not have
many responsibilities in the world.
To live a simple and happy life,
grateful for the little things.

Julia Garcia, age 15

This song about a lovestruck girl and her romantically naïve best friend was written at the WriteGirl Songwriting Workshop.

Love Angst

You tell me, "It's okay"
When it's not
You tell me, "Everything's all right"
When it never will be
You try to protect me
When you're defenseless
You say you forgive me
When you were never upset
You laugh because you're arguing
Just to push my buttons

Your smirk erases me
Your gaze evades me

Don't smile because my scowl amuses you
Don't lie when you say,
"Love is beyond you"
Because I love you
I do
Even if you can't say it, too

Amaya McGinnis, age 18

The Curtain

The girl dances behind the curtain
Her shadow plays on the deep red fabric
She watches as shadowed lights flash
And a wondrous voice fills the room

Her body sways to the muffled music
She closes her eyes and imagines silk and beads covering her
She doesn't hide behind the curtain
She's the star

She dazzles the gasping crowd
Wonder and amazement light their faces
as her hair falls to her shoulders
Suddenly the music stops and the applause roars
"Encore" they shout!
And she gives it to them
Leaps, twirls, shaking hips
The music moves her and she dances all her pain away

She hasn't heard her own laughter in years
But it flows through her now
And soon she can't stop
She falls to the ground in a dizzy heap
But then she opens her eyes
Looks down at her ragged clothing
Feels her tied-up hair and the broom in her hands

She's frozen mid-dance
To music no longer playing
The song has ended
Happiness disappears
Reality comes
The curtain has closed.

Arrive late – leave early – in the scene, That is.

Kamryn Alina Barker, age 17

Move On

Stop singing that same sad song
over and over
Stop humming that tune
We've all sung our fair share of sad songs

You shut your ears to sweet melodies
You keep singing about the dark,
about the horrors of your life,
the gloom that fills your heart
You sing that same dreary song
as you wake up
and when you go to sleep
It stops you from living life

Stop singing that song
Put your head to the sky
Gather the strength to move on

Isabel Gil, age 17

*I wanted to write about the moment when you realize you are
no longer under a person's spell.*

A Random Page

I turn, and there you are, with that run-down acoustic guitar you
named Grace, the only woman that you'll ever pour your heart out
to. I stroll on, by your side, and half-trip on my self-pity – as I lean
down to pick up the belongings I dropped, you immediately take
hold of my heavily-rubbed quotebook, a diary of sorts.

You tear it open to a random page – oddly enough, the very one
that I'm ashamed of. Scrawled across the page is the song that you
showed me, and that I fell in love with. You see the embarrassment
pour across my face, and for once, without question, you simply
begin to play it.

Soon, we're both melodiously singing,
> *And I got to the point where all I wanted was for us
> to make up but it's not that easy, 'cause girl, you move
> on so quickly…*

For a moment, it feels like old times. But of course, with me being
overly caught up in the moment, I gaze into your eyes, and I don't
even realize we're not alone until Blake butts in, "Your guys' voices
sound really nice together…" I politely smile and say thanks, instead
of blurting out all of the things that are in my head. I simply walk,
aloof, into the night air with a twinkle in my eye, and a beautiful
feeling of freedom.

14 people & places

a german accent
on the
HORIZON

Mayra Sebastian, age 16

This piece was inspired by a picture of a curious little baby that my mentor, Vicky, got from a magazine. We started by just describing the baby and it turned into this poem.

I Exist

Chubby, cotton soft face,
Intrigued, surprised.
Light bulb bright eyes,
Hands, teeny and gentle.

Innocence in his soul,
Black and blonde bumble bee hair,
Elf ears, a little too titanic for his head.

Perfectly centered rabbit tail nose,
Itty-bitty lips – stretching tremendously for the world.
Eyebrows barely noticeable,
That say, "I exist."

Allison Deegan, mentor

Vienna

There is a place set for you
At the table in Vienna
Water glass to one side
Notepaper, logo pens
With everyone you gathered
Consumed by preparation
Predicting the end of the world

There is a street, any street
On one of seven continents
Where you learned to survive
Getting along, asking questions
With everyone you gathered
Fueled by imagination
Fearing the end of the world

There is a city below the hills
Littered with castaways and gold
You made it there, you drank well
Embracing greatness at last
With everyone you gathered
Commanding full attention
Preventing the end of the world

There is a place set for you
At the table in Vienna
Preventing the end the world

Tracy DeBrincat, mentor

During a mentoring session, we wrote about mysterious neighbors.
My grandmother's neighborhood was an exciting, unknown world
to be conquered.

The Neighbor

When the fog creeps in, the house across the street from my
grandmother's almost disappears. It, too, is the color of mist.

With window shades like clouds and a front stoop that melts into
sidewalk, the border between structure and street evaporates.

The man inside, Fritz, has blanched, indoor skin and a salted
moustache. He wears soft leather gloves and shoes the color
of doves.

Sunday mornings, he blooms in a green wool fedora. A martini
olive of a hat, with a ruby bird feather and burgundy ribbon.

Afternoons, he pulls on a one-piece grey jumpsuit and knee-high
rubber boots to wax and buff his pearly Packard in the drive.

Once he brought us sugar-dusted Christmas treats wrapped in wax
paper. His German accent was so thick, I couldn't understand what
he was saying.

When my grandmother said, "Thank you," he reached for her
hand and kissed it. We saw that his eyes were bright blue.

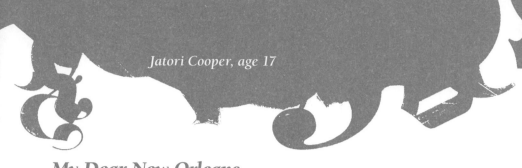

Jatori Cooper, age 17

My Dear New Orleans

Mosquitos fly in the hot and humid weather
Sometimes I wake up and find
that they have left their red itchy marks on my calves
My mom continuously tells me not to scratch
And I continuously do the opposite

That Southern hospitality always brings me back:
Two parts delicious
Five parts festive

Join in with the jazz band
Tap your foot or clap your hands
It's hard to hang your head low or keep to yourself

Get in the mix with the Mardi Gras celebration
Happiness and beads are everywhere

For family gatherings,
New Orleans has my heart
She will forever be my birthplace

Treat her nicely, if you please
And enjoy your stay in My Dear New Orleans

Antonia Crane, mentor

This was a non-fiction exercise using all the senses.

Rooms I Have Known: Folsom Street Yellow

My Folsom Street apartment was a dark, barnlike Victorian with an unfinished wood floor and loud plumbing that shook the walls. When the old pipes rattled, the hidden ironing board shook loose from its nook and fell open with a startling thud. The wood floor was impossible to keep clean, even though I swept and mopped. The antiseptic Pine-Sol smell seeped in and lingered.

I liked to sit on the dusty dark floor with my journal. I'd always wanted a red kitchen, but was told red would start fights. I chose bright cherry red paint and hung gingham curtains to match. I decorated it with vintage aprons and used 70s dishes from Valencia Street shops. My vibrant red kitchen was a place of whistling kettles, striped cat mugs and no fights.

My room was robin's egg blue, nearly turquoise, a relentlessly cheerful sky in the wet, grey city. To brighten it, I chose a soft sunflower color for the mock fireplace. It was a pale yellow that popped like lemon meringue – sugar, egg whites, and vanilla. Later, yellow became an intrusive flashing light, the sign of cancer and later, the astonished blaze of death.

When I uncurled years later, I knew the brutish yellow of rebirth. Every egg I cracked in my red kitchen reminded me of my mother's neighbor, the one with the chickens – who noticed her turn yellow before the cancer. My one window had a view: concrete – the space between my house and the apartment building next door. At night, my neighbors screamed at each other in one high shrill pitch. I wondered how they could breathe while screaming like that – a screeching, yellow cry. Their chainsaw voices gave me recurring sound dreams of a rhythmic thwack – the beating of wings.

Valerie Howard, mentor

This poem was part of a longer journal entry I wrote one evening after I spent the entire day surfing.

Surfing

The scenes of my house beckon me,
Tugging at my shirt,
Like random piles of dirty clothes
Strewn across the floor,
The unopened bills calling my name,
And the plants in need of watering.
The list goes on and on and on,
But I don't care today
Because the world beckons, too
And dirty dishes no longer matter
When there is surfing to do.

Jessica McCarthy, mentor

Time and Travel

We were in my boyfriend's homeland, a place still scarred by the destruction of a decade-old civil war, evidenced by the bombed out buildings and half-built homes that dot the landscape. New NATO borders meant the town his father was born into now belongs to another country with a new nationality that none here are willing to claim. Theirs was a legacy that withstood such things: war, displacement, persecution. Now, they cling to their land and identity with fervor.

Following lunch at his uncle's house, my boyfriend is eager to share everything about the little town and its history that he can with me. Just down the road, hidden amongst pastures and family farms, lies a small fenced in plot of land, immaculately kept and filled with concrete saints, marble benches, and wind worn headstones. I tiptoe between the graves and I glance at the different spans of years. Doing quick calculations in my head, I find myself thinking, "She lived a good, long life" or "Oh, what a shame."

The gray stone at my feet is etched with my boyfriend's name. Suddenly, I am 92 years old, my skin thin and translucent, with wiry white hair blowing against my black dress. The land that I am standing on falls away and I am looking down at an abyss, which has claimed my beloved. In that moment, I feel a great sense of what it means to be "without" and how little time I have left to love him.

I make a beeline for the road, trying desperately to force back tears. Catching up with me, perhaps thinking I had been spooked, he nervously asks, "Sorry. Was that weird?"

Sarine Balian, mentor

Church

Incense-smoked air, light from
windows up high catch glimmers
cold insulated by warmly dressed bodies
side by side
stale dry communion and a drop or two of
wine, melting, dissipating
choir on- and off-balance singing
hears, self-consciousness
clergy chanting, mumbling ancient text
mind drifts from boredom, to fantasies, to wonder
of goings-on behind the curtains
if it could be quiet enough for a moment
you'd hear God

McKenzie Givens, age 16

This piece is a response to a depressing book I was reading. The author's world was so foreboding and melancholic, I felt the need to write and escape.

Lost Highway

I'm on a road trip to infinity. Nothing but miles & miles of empty highway between me & eternity. A sprawling expanse of desert ripples, untamed in the heat of the day, disappears into the evening like an extinguished candle. A lonesome, broken yellow line: the only barrier between life & death & all the rest.

Beneath the smothering hand of the starry night, primordial phantoms ooze between my fluid newborn dreams. "Come play with us," they wail. But I opt for black coffee & an apple pie in some ancient atomic diner left open for the midnight prowlers, the sleepless howlers, the broken, shuddering shadows of men & the blissful intimations of Zen. The waitress jumps at every sign of life & the furniture slumps with every patron's sigh. I look around at all the faceless gods, buzzing away beneath the red neon glow of *Open All Night* and *Made Fresh Daily*.

The galaxies of grease in my cup remind me to keep on searching. I turn back to the sweltering night with its electric air & continue past some rogue buildings crumbling into the barren landscape. Mostly Half-Moon Motels, vacancies shimmering in the night. A few more diners for the detritus of day.

The seconds drift by. Dragging along minutes. Hours. A few solemn years. Just as I begin to forget what sunlight tastes like, the hopeful glow of morning appears on the horizon: the youthful, yawning blue rising from the depths of the earth. The volatile wisps of lilac & rose. The uncoiling rivers of light. The timeless glitter of dew in its final moment. The convulsive eruptions of bittersweet vermilion & saffron.

This *is* Write Girl

"WriteGirl has been a gateway to freedom. When I write, I feel free. It's just the pen, the paper, and me and I feel in control."

– a WriteGirl mentee

This is writeGirl

Founded in 2001, WriteGirl is a creative writing and mentoring organization for teen girls. WriteGirl serves over 300 teen girls in Los Angeles County.

In its Core Mentoring Program, girls attend from 86 schools. WriteGirl pairs teen girls with professional women writers for one-on-one mentoring, workshops, public readings and publication in award-winning, nationally-distributed anthologies. This anthology is the eleventh publication from WriteGirl's Core Mentoring Program. WriteGirl also provides individual college and financial aid guidance to every participant. For the eleventh year in a row, 100% of teens participating in the WriteGirl Core Mentoring Program have graduated from high school and enrolled in college.

WriteGirl also brings weekly creative writing workshops to more than 150 critically at-risk teen girls at through its innovative In-Schools Program. The WriteGirl In-Schools Program, launched in 2004, currently serves four Los Angeles County Office of Education schools in the communities of Lawndale, Azusa, South Los Angeles, and Santa Clarita. Three of the schools are Community Day Schools. Students at these schools are pregnant or parenting teens, foster youth, on probation, have social workers or are unable to return to their home schools due to any number of issues. The fourth school is the Road to Success Academy in Santa Clarita at Camp Scott and Camp Scudder, adjacent juvenile detention facilities.

Through positive, caring role models, girls learn to share their work and express their feelings in a diverse community of women and peers.

Through participation in WriteGirl, girls develop vital communication skills, self confidence, critical thinking skills, deeper academic engagement and enhanced creativity for a lifetime of increased opportunities.

"WriteGirl is a place I come to be free and to be me." – a WriteGirl mentee

"I love the spirit of adventure and fearlessness."
— a WriteGirl mentor

The WriteGirl community is positive, supportive and highly contagious!

WriteGirl teens are encouraged to share their work at public readings, workshops and special events.

WriteGirl mentors are accomplished novelists, journalists, poets, songwriters, screenwriters, marketing professionals and more.

MentORiNg

WriteGirl matches professional women writers with teen girls for one-on-one mentoring in creative writing. Every week, mentoring pairs meet at coffee shops, libraries, museums or other creative locations. They write, reflect and inspire each other. WriteGirl screens, selects and trains women writers to prepare them to be effective writing mentors. Mentor advisors provide support and help throughout the year. 150 women writers contribute 2,000 volunteer hours each month as mentors, workshop leaders and volunteers.

Mentors guide girls throughout the college application process. For eleven years in row, 100% of participating WriteGirl seniors have gone on to college.

"My mentee's writing voice keeps getting stronger. A joy to witness." – a WriteGirl mentor

"Such a huge rainbow of feelings, and stories, and brilliant notions!"

– a WriteGirl mentee

WriteGirl pairs work together for an average of three years. Many mentors stay in touch with their mentees throughout their college years and beyond.

At WriteGirl, mentoring works both ways. Mentors and mentees learn from and inspire each other.

WORKSHOPS

One Saturday each month throughout the nine-month season, WriteGirl teens and women writers gather for a full day of writing. Workshops are led by professional women novelists, poets, screenwriters, songwriters, and journalists. They are some of the most respected writers in their fields. WriteGirl partners with prestigious institutions throughout the city, such as the GRAMMY museum, Los Angeles Times and MOCA to provide exciting venues for these innovative workshops.

Workshops are intensive, interactive and jam-packed with fresh writing activities and special guest presenters.

Many of the pieces found in this book started out as WriteGirl workshop experiments.

"I loved meeting a girl who came to her first WriteGirl workshop and gathered the courage to share her work for the first time."

– a WriteGirl mentor

"Today, I loved my apple juice box, my encouraging mentor who likes cheese like me, and the moment of confidence."

– a WriteGirl mentee

At the Songwriting Workshop, guest singer/songwriters guide girls to write lyrics, then set them to music at the end of the day.

Monthly workshops bring together a diverse group of women and girls, building lasting relationships and a uniquely vibrant community.

Special Guest Presenters & Mentors

Poetry Workshop:
Linda J. Albertano
Laurel Ann Bogen

Fiction Workshop:
Katie Alender
Marlys West

Character & Dialogue Workshop:

Script Doctors:
Jane Anderson
Loraine Despres
Liz Sarnoff
Jacqueline Wilson
Melissa Wong

Actors:
Bryn Abbot
Kamar de los Reyes
Khalilah Dubose
Fernanda Espindola
Jarvis George
Porter Kelly
Retta Putignano King
Lovelle Liquigan
Florencia Lozano
Matt Palazzolo
Sherri Saum
Lisa Singer
Ryan Smith
Erwin Tuazon
Leah Yananton

"I loved the excitement and encouragement that all girls showed to each other." – a Guest

Journalism panel at the Los Angeles Times auditorium.

"I always get really excited and inspired at WriteGirl workshops. I love being around all these talented, smart women." – a WriteGirl mentee

Songwriting Workshop:

Danielle Brisebois
Kyler England
Nina Gordon
Kay Hanley
Libby Lavella
Michelle Lewis
Clare Means

Eve Nelson
Holly Palmer
Simone Porter
Lindsay Rush
Lucy Schwartz
Keren Taylor

Journalism Workshop:

Aida Ahmad
Stephanie Becker
Carey Bodenheimer
Jen Jones Donatelli
Mona Gable
Colleen Wainwright

Literary Panel at Mentor Retreat:

Monica Faulkner
Jamie Fitzgerald
Jennie Nash
Colleen Wainwright

Performance Workshop:

Porter Kelly
Leah Yananton

Poet Laurel Ann Bogen guides girls through dynamic poetry writing activities.

The Songwriting Workshop culminated in performances by singer/songwriters in the GRAMMY museum's Clive Davis Theater.

Public Readings

WriteGirl teens read their work boldly at bookstores, theaters and book festivals all over the city. Their performances never fail to entertain and inspire.

Performing at large public events like the Los Angeles Times Festival of Books and the West Hollywood Book Fair develops confidence.

"The courage of the WriteGirl teens to share their voice is outstanding."
– a WriteGirl mentor

> *"I loved hearing the girls reading aloud – it gave me part of my youth back."*
> – a WriteGirl mentor

Each nine-month WriteGirl season culminates in a high-energy celebration at the Writers Guild of America Theater in Beverly Hills. The event features a silent auction, lunch reception, special celebrity guests and a sneak preview of the next WriteGirl anthology.

BoLD INk awards

The annual WriteGirl Bold Ink Awards were created to honor the women who inspire our girls, our mentors and audiences around the world. We seek out storytellers whose voices move us. Their genres represent the breadth of our own membership and their achievements mark the degree of excellence we all strive for. They write in Bold Ink.

Honoree Kara DioGuardi (Ain't No Other Man, Walk Away, Undo It) at the 2011 Bold Ink Awards

2011 Honoree Nia Vardalos (My Big Fat Greek Wedding, I Hate Valentine's Day) accepts her Bold Ink Award

Past Bold Ink Award Honorees:

Aline Brosh McKenna
Wanda Coleman
Jennifer Crittenden
Diablo Cody
Liz Craft
Kara DioGuardi
Savannah Dooley
Sarah Fain
Janet Fitch
Carol Flint
Naomi Foner
Winnie Holzman
Gigi Levangie
Callie Khouri
Suzanne Lummis
Nancy Meyers
Patt Morrison
Carol Muske-Dukes
Sonia Nazario
Gina Prince-Bythewood
Lynda Resnick
Elizabeth Sarnoff
Carolyn See
Patricia Seyburn
Marisa Silver
Sarah Silverman
Mona Simpson
Jill Soloway
Robin Swicord
Sandra Tsing Loh
Nia Vardalos
Diane Warren

Honoree Jennifer Crittenden, television writer and producer, at the 2009 Bold Ink Awards

PubliCatiOns

Since 2001, WriteGirl Publications has been producing award-winning anthologies that showcase the bold voices and imaginative insights of women and girls. Unique in both design and content, WriteGirl anthologies present a wide range of personal stories, poetry, essays, scenes and lyrics. WriteGirl inspires readers to find their own creative voices through innovative writing experiments and writing tips from both teens and their mentors.

Eleven anthologies from WriteGirl feature the work of over 1,000 women and girls. Selections range from serious to whimsical, personal to political, and heart-rending to uplifting.

WriteGirl anthologies have collectively won more than 40 national and international book awards!

- Order WriteGirl books from **www.WriteGirl.org**, **www.Amazon.com**, or bookstores nationwide.

- *ForeWord Reviews, School Library Journal, Kirkus, Los Angeles Times Book Review, The Writer Magazine* and *VOYA* have all raved about WriteGirl books.

"Girls passionate about writing is what carries this book...This is a great anniversary edition and will inspire other teens with its creativity and passion."
– Eric Hoffer Award Committee, Honorable Mention for "Intensity," Young Adult Category

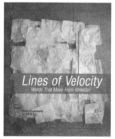
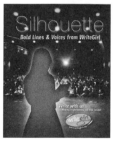

Pens on Fire, WriteGirl's educator's guide, offers over 200 inspiring writing experiments for teens and adults. Through the innovative use of props, movement, art, music, textures, scents and even flavors, *Pens on Fire* offers step-by-step creative writing curricula for teachers and youth leaders.

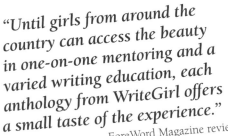

"Until girls from around the country can access the beauty in one-on-one mentoring and a varied writing education, each anthology from WriteGirl offers a small taste of the experience."
— ForeWord Magazine review

"Write on Girls: yours are the voices that must be read."
— a WriteGirl mentor

"Love these young minds and all the treasures in their brains."
— a WriteGirl mentor

bold Futures

WriteGirl develops leaders. The WriteGirl Bold Futures Program weaves together a full slate of college and job preparedness skill building, as well as leadership development to truly give young women the tools, community, confidence and tenacious communication skills they need to thrive, in college, in the workplace and in life. The Bold Futures Program offers intensive opportunities for high school seniors and college students to participate on planning committees, at special events and as interns in the WriteGirl office.

WriteGirl teens have won creative writing awards from the City of Los Angeles Department of Cultural Affairs and The Sally Picow Foundation.

"WriteGirl and all of its amazing members are a fantastic tribute to the power of women. Thank you for helping to make it a reality!"
— a WriteGirl alumna

WriteGirl has developed strong partnerships with a broad range of companies to help girls envision future careers.

"WriteGirl was a great start without a finish because once you're a WriteGirl, you're a WriteGirl for life."

– a WriteGirl alumna

WriteGirl alumnae are entering the workforce as creative, motivated college grads eager to give back.

"Every amazing, life-changing experience I've had so far is somehow tied back to WG because it catalyzed my personal growth."

– a WriteGirl alumna

Praise for WriteGirl

Never underestimate the power of a girl and her pen!

From mentees:

"The best feeling in the world is when people laugh at the words I write."
— a WriteGirl mentee

"I was lost, confused, and completely in the dark about what to do! But now I am on the right path, WriteGirl."
— a WriteGirl mentee

"I'm happy to be here. I don't feel shy anymore. I've learned how to express myself more."
— a WriteGirl mentee

From mentors:

"I loved listening to my mentee's words and how she crafted a story."
— a WriteGirl mentor

"Oh, what a marvelous, righteous, fabulous generation of girls they are. ONWARD!"
— a WriteGirl mentor

"The quiet ones always impress me with their bravery and imagination."
— a WriteGirl mentor

"I realized my daughter is seen and known and supported by WriteGirl in a profound way." – a WriteGirl parent

"I've seen my daughter go from shy to blossoming. Before, she would sit in the back of the class. You could never get her on stage. Also, she really wants to write more. She's inspired." – a WriteGirl parent

"I now understand what a positive experience it is for my daughter to be in WriteGirl. It is the best experience she could have." – a WriteGirl parent

From teachers:

"This program needs to be in every school. WriteGirl has a unique approach that gets results." – a teacher

Leadership: The WriteGirl "Engine"

Executive Director
Keren Taylor

Associate Director
Allison Deegan

Workshops Coordinator
Kirsten Giles

In-Schools Program Coordinator
Brande Jackson

Events Manager
Jessica McCarthy

Silent Auctions
Retta Putignano

Administrative & Event Assistants
Leslie Awender
Naomi Buckley
Cindy Collins
Sylvia Grossman
Rachel Hogue
Lindsay Mendoza
Staci Roberts
Shilloy Sanchez

WriteGirl College and Alumnae Interns
Dulce Castrejon
Lauren Sarazen

High School Interns
Mari Flores
Jenny Gonzalez
Special thanks to the *Constitutional Rights Foundation* for the placement and supervision of committed teens interning with WriteGirl.

Website, Branding, Book Design, Graphics
Sara Apelkvist
Erin Fleiner
Nathalie Gallmeier
Juliana Sankaran-Felix
Velvette De Laney

Photography/Videography
Lisa Beebe
Lindsay Boyce
Clayton Goodfellow
Thomas Hargis
Margaret Hyde
Apple Price
Mario de Lopez
Marvin Yan

WriteGirl staff and board members guide program development and financial sustainability.

WriteGirl Board:

John Marshall: Vice President-Manufacturing, RR Donnelley, global provider of integrated communications (Board Chair)

Allison Deegan: Public Education Administrator, Ed.D (Strategic Planning Chair)

Nandita Patel: Procurement Executive, The Walt Disney Company

Maria del Pilar O'Cadiz: Project Scientist, Department of Education, UC Irvine

Keren Taylor: Songwriter, Poet, Visual Artist (WriteGirl Founder and Executive Director)

Sydney Zhang: The Capitol Group

Advisory Board:

Barbara Abercrombie: Novelist, UCLA Writing Instructor, Lecturer

Shelley Berger: Poet and Beyond Baroque Poetry Teacher

Mark Bisgeier: Entertainment Attorney

Susie Coelho: Lifestyle Expert, Author and HGTV Television Host

Mark E. Cull: Author and Publisher, Red Hen Press

Paul Cummins: Executive Director, New Visions Foundation

Kai EL' Zabar: Writer, Editor, Multimedia Consultant

Elizabeth Forsythe Hailey: Novelist

Mollie Gregory: Author, Teacher, Consultant for Writers

Vickie Nam: Writer, Editor of Yell-Oh Girls (Asian-American teen anthology), Interactive Producer

Joy Picus: Former LA Councilwoman and Community Organizer

Debbie Reber: Author

Aleida Rodríguez: Poet, Editor, Educator, Translator, Publisher

Diane Siegel: Museum Educator, Community Organizer, Teacher, Los Angeles Public Library Consultant

Community Connections

Participating Schools:

Alliance College Ready Academy # 7

Albert Einstein Academy

Alverno High School

Anahuacalmecac University Preparatory High School

Animo Pat Brown School

Arcadia High School

Aspire Pacific Academy

Azusa High School

Bell High School

Benjamin Franklin High School

Blair High School - An International Baccalaureate World School

Bolsa Grande High School

Bright Star Secondary Charter Academy

CALS Early College High School

CHAMPS Charter High School of the Arts

Culver City High School

Dana Middle School

Daniel Pearl Magnet High School

Dr. Walter C. Ralston Intermediate School

El Segundo Middle School

Film and Theatre Arts Charter High School

Foothill Country Day School

Frederick Douglass Academy

Gabrielino High School

Garden Grove High

Gardena High School

Garvey Junior High School

Hamilton High School

Hamilton High School Academy of Music

Harvard-Westlake

Highland Hall Waldorf School

Hollywood High School

Huntington Beach High

Huntington Park High School

International Polytechnic High School

Immaculate Heart High School

International Studies Learning Center

James A. Foshay Learning Center

John Burroughs Middle School

John Marshall High School

Juan Rodriquez Cabrillo High School

King Drew Magnet High School of Medicine and Science

La Habra High School

Lakewood Christian Schools

Laurel Hall School

Los Angeles Center For Enriched Studies

Los Angeles Leadership Academy

Los Angeles Unified Alternative Education School

Los Osos High School

Lynwood High School

Manual Arts Senior High School

Mark Keppel High

Marlborough School

Marymount High School

Metropolitan High School

Middle College High School

Miguel Contreras Learning Complex

New Village Charter School

North Hollywood High School

Notre Dame High School

Opportunities for Learning

Options for Youth

Orange County High School of the Arts

Orchard Hills High School

Palisades Charter High School

Port of Los Angeles High Schools

Providence High School

Ramon C. Cortines School Of Visual And Performing Arts

Robert F. Kennedy Community Schools

San Fernando Valley High School

San Marino High School

Sandburg Middle School

Southeast High School

St. Lucy's Priory High School

St. Mary's Academy

Sunland Christian School

Sussman Middle School

Temple City High School

Toll Middle School/Hoover High School

Ulysses S. Grant High School

University High School

Valley Alternative Magnet School

Venice High School

Walter Reed Middle School

Whittier High School

Wildwood School

Referring Organizations:

Antioch University Los Angeles

Constitutional Rights Foundation

Fox Gives

Idealist

Los Angeles Times Festival of Books

PEN Center USA West

UCLA Extension Writers' Program

United Way of Ventura

VolunteerMatch

West Hollywood Book Fair

Writers Guild of America, West

WriteGirl Supporters

WriteGirl would like to thank all of our individual donors who have so generously contributed to help us grow and help more teen girls each year.

WriteGirl would like to extend a very special thank you to **Colleen Wainwright** for her generosity and inspiring creativity. Her "50 for 50" campaign garnered support for WriteGirl from people all over the country and gave us the momentum we needed to take us to the next level. Much gratitude for all the "50 for 50" supporters, with a special thank you to the following:

67 Robots

Authentic Consulting

Barry Schwartz Photography

Bee Franck Designs

Chris Glass Design

Danielle LaPorte

Daring Fireball

Donna Barger Illustration

Field Notes

Good Job!

Josh Ross Creative

Molly Bryant Music

Mule Design

parlato design studio

Ruby Calling

Shawn G. Henry Photographer

Smile Software

The Art of Non-Conformity

The Jason Womack Company

The World-Changing Writing Workshop

Tokyo Farm

TonyOnTheWeb

W.I.B. Videos

Wayne M. DeSelle Design

Your Big, Beautiful Book Plan

Thank you, Colleen, from all of us at WriteGirl.

We would also like to thank the following foundations, government entities, and corporations for their support:

AAUW Educational Foundation

Adams Family Foundation

Allied Integrated Marketing

Amazon.com

Annenberg Foundation

Araca Group

ASCAP Foundation

Band From TV

California Community Foundation

Citrin Cooperman and Company

City of Los Angeles Department of Cultural Affairs

Cosmic Hooker

Crail Johnson Foundation

Creative Artists Agency

Do You Zoom

Dwight Stuart Youth Foundation

Edlow Family Fund

Elizabeth George Foundation

Five For Fairness

Fox Group

Fur Ball Inc.

Girl Friday Films Inc.

Good News Foundation

Good Works Foundation

Green Foundation

iGive

Human Family Educational and Cultural Institute

Jennifer Louden Inc.

JR Hyde III Family Foundation

Juju Technologies Corp

Los Angeles County Office of Education

Los Angeles Unified School District Beyond the Bell

Marc & Eva Stern Foundation

Marlborough Student Charitable Fund of The Women's Foundation of California

Metafilter

Mule Design Studio

NBC Universal

Oder Family Foundation

Paradigm

Ralph M Parsons Foundation

Ralphs

Roll International

Rose Hills Foundation

RR Donnelley

Skirball Foundation

State Street Foundation

Sun Life Financial

Thruline Entertainment

Twentieth Century Fox Film Corporation

United Talent Agency

William Morris Endeavor

Women Helping Youth

Woohoo Inc.

Ziffren Brittenham LLP

Our Special Thanks To

All of WriteGirl's mentors and volunteers for professional services, including strategic planning, public relations, event coordination, mentoring management, training & curriculum development, catering, financial management and administrative assistance.

Advisory Board Members for their support and guidance on strategy, fundraising, communications and development of community partnerships.

The Honorable Mayor Antonio Villaraigosa; Los Angeles Council President Eric Garcetti, Los Angeles Council members Tom LaBonge and **Jan Perry**; for their support and acknowledgement of WriteGirl's contributions to the community.

Los Angeles Unified School District, Beyond the Bell Division and the Miguel Contreras Learning Center, GRAMMY® Foundation, GRAMMY® Museum, Los Angeles Times, MOCA, Volunteer Assistance League of Southern California and the **Writers Guild of America** for helping provide event space.

Book Expo America, Los Angeles Times Festival of Books, Skylight Books, West Hollywood Book Fair, and **UCLA Writers Faire** for donating WriteGirl space and promotional support at these events.

Fabric Interactive and Sara Apelkvist for design and branding strategy, including development of WriteGirl's logo, website, press kit, stationery, publications and ongoing support.

Writing Journals: Anne McGilvray & Company, Blick Art Materials, BrushDance Inc., Carolina Pads, Cavallini Papers & Co., Chronicle Books, Ecojot, Falling Water, Fiorentina, Flavia, Galison/MudPuppy Press, Harry Abrams, Hartley and Marks, JournalBooks, Kikkerland Design, Michael Roger Press, Mirage Paper Company, Paperblanks, Quotable Cards, Retired Hipster, Rock Scissor Paper, Running Rhino & Co., K. Schweitzer, Trends International, Whimsy Press.

Food, Dessert and Beverages at WriteGirl Workshops and Special Events: Bagel Broker, Barefoot Wine & Bubbly, Barragan's Mexican Restaurant, Big Sugar Bakeshop, Border Grill, Brooklyn Bagel Bakery, Carol Martin Cupcakes, Chipotle, Cookie Casa, Corner Bakery, Earth Wind and Flour, El Pollo Loco, Frankie's on Melrose, Homeboy Industries, Hubert's Lemonade, IZZE Beverages, Kychon Chicken, La Pizza Loca, Les Macarons Duverger, Little Caesar's Pizza, Louise's Trattoria, Mani's Bakery, Masa of Echo Park, Michael's Restaurant, Mozza, Musso and Franks, Nestlé Juicy Juice, Nickel Diner, Numero Uno Pizza, Olive Garden, Panda Restaurant Group, Panera Bread, Paramount Farms, Pescado Mojado, Platine Cookies, POM Wonderful, Porto's Bakery, Ralphs, Real Food Daily, Sharky's Woodfired Mexican Grill, Señor Fish, Spitz, Starbucks, Street, SusieCakes, The Riverside Café, Trader Joe's, TRU Vodka, Tudor House, Veggie Grill, Whole Foods Market, Yuca's and all of our volunteers who donated delicious desserts.

Gifts for Members and Event Donors: ABC Family, ASCAP, Bambola Beauty, Boo Boo Bling, Daisy Rock Guitar, DIRECTV, Earthly Body, Earthpack, Evan Healy Cosmetics, FACE Stockholm, FedEx Office, Finders Key Purse, Fox Gives, Fox Home Entertainment, Fox Searchlight, Get Fresh, Glee Gum, Granta, Hint Mints, KiNeSYS, KPR, Lance Christopher, Lipsi Cosmetics, MOCA, Mo's Nose, NBC Universal, NYX, Parlux Fragrances Inc., Quotable Cards, Soolip Paperie, Teleflora, The Good Cheer Company, The GRAMMY Museum, Wonderful Pistachios, Yogi Tea.

Printing and Copy Services: Chromatic Lithographers Inc., FedEx Office, RR Donnelley.

Publicity and Marketing: BlogHer Network, Mamapalooza.

Meet the WriteGirl Mentors

Maia Akiva is a magical realism writer, originally from Israel. Her plays have had readings all over the USA, and her short stories, sketches and a one-act play were published in magazines. You can find her at www.maiaakiva.com.

Abby Anderson is an award-winning screenwriter, whose scripts have placed in the Top 5% in the Nicholl Fellowship. She is very proud of her mentee, Jessica, who is in her second year studying screenwriting at Cal State Fullerton and is off on a Central American adventure this summer on a Semester at Sea!

Jane Anderson is a screenwriter, playwright and film director. Her plays have been produced Off-Broadway and in theaters around the country. Her film and TV work has won her some nice statuary. WriteGirl keeps her sane. Hurrah!

Sarine Balian is a writer and musician, living in Los Angeles. She volunteers with the WriteGirl In-Schools program.

Lisa Beebe blogs and writes personality quizzes for TeenNick.com. She is working on her first YA novel, and dreams of one day being a special guest at WriteGirl's annual fiction workshop.

Annie Brown, an East Coast transplant, is working to grow her educational consulting business. This year, she has thrown other work aside to plunge into writing a book for new teachers based on her twelve years' experience teaching history and English.

Julie Buchwald is a full-time investigator, working for the Office of the Inspector General. She conducts civilian oversight of LAPD officer-involved shootings. In her free time, Julie is an accomplished triathlete and tries, tries, tries to work on her novel. Julie loves working with all the amazing and brilliant WriteGirls.

Naomi Buckley holds an MFA in Sculpture and has exhibited throughout the country and internationally. She currently is a master teacher at the Armory Center for the Arts. Naomi is also an RYT at the 200-hour level and teaches yoga and mindfulness meditation. She is currently working on her MA in Psychology with an emphasis in Spiritual and Depth Psychology.

Liz Campanile is an MFA student studying Creative Non-Fiction. She's been published in *Working World* magazine and California Psychics online and makes a lot of sarcastic comments on Twitter @ Adora2000. You can also find her blog at http://cookingwithaphrodite.blogspot.com/

Kathleen Cecchin is an actor, director and playwright. Her play *Bitch* was published in a collection of pieces entitled *Can I Sit With You?* She helps create WriteGirl workshop handouts. Her favorite workshop is Songwriting, because she doesn't know how to do it.

Cindy Collins writes short stories, scripts and Web content. She has a background in television production and graduated from the University of Arizona with a degree in Journalism. This is her sixth season as a WriteGirl volunteer.

Jia-Rui Cook is a science writer and media relations specialist at NASA's Jet Propulsion Laboratory. She gets to write about exotic, smoggy moons and ice volcanoes for a living. In the past, she has written for the *Los Angeles Times* and *Newsweek*.

Antonia Crane is a California Native. Her work can be found on The Rumpus, Black Clock, Slake, ZYZZYVA, Word Riot, PANK, *The Los Angeles Review*, *Smith Magazine*, and other places. She teaches Creative Writing to teenagers after school in Los Angeles.

Tracy DeBrincat's debut novel, *Hollywood Buckaroo*, was published in 2012 by Black Lawrence Press. A fiction collection, *Moon Is Cotton & She Laugh All Night*, was published in 2010. Her stories and poetry have appeared widely in literary reviews.

Vicky Deger is originally from the beaches of Sydney, Australia. Vicky's work has appeared in or is forthcoming in *The Coachella Review*, *The Grove Review* and *Gulf Stream Magazine*. She lives in Los Angeles, where she has raised two young men and works as a costume designer.

Kim Derby is a freelance writer, most recently for *Dwell*. Prior to that, she contributed design, art and architecture content for *EcoSalon*. She did her graduate studies in Interior & Architectural Design at UCLA and is currently working on her first book, a memoir.

Loraine Despres has written screenplays, pilots and numerous TV episodes, including the "Who Shot J.R.?" episode of *Dallas*. She has taught screenwriting at UCLA and her first novel, *The Scandalous Summer of Sissy Leblanc*, was a national bestseller.

Caitlin Dube is a poet, writer, and aspiring doctor. An East Coast transplant, Caitlin taught literature and writing in New York before moving to Los Angeles. She has begun pre-medical studies and hopes to continue working with all the wonderful WriteGirls.

Elaine Dutka is freelance writer and contributing reporter at KUSC, National Public Radio. A former staff writer for the *Los Angeles Times* and West Coast Show Business Correspondent for *Time Magazine*, she was part of a team of Pulitzer Prize finalists and has won two LA Press Club Awards.

Amanda Elend is a new media writer/producer who loves her animals as if they were children. You can follow her on Twitter @amandaelend if you enjoy wasting time as much as she does.

Julie Ershadi is a journalist and a lifelong writer. She is from Los Angeles, but might have a Pennsylvanian soul. She has been blessed by her experience with WriteGirl this year.

Rachel Fain is a freelance writer and editor, and has worked for 20 years in LA theatre. She did an 11-year stint at Center Theatre Group, where she created nearly three dozen play guides for students and adults. www.rachelgfain.com; http://www.lastagetimes.com/author/rachelfain/

Susanne Ferrull has worked as a journalist, editor, publicist, corporate communicator and freelance writer for more than 20 years, specializing in travel and entertainment. She holds a Masters degree in Journalism from Syracuse University.

In addition to being a five-year veteran mentor with WriteGirl, **Linda Folsom** is the proud parent of WriteGirl alumna, Alana, who will graduate this year with a BA in Creative Writing from Bates College.

Dina Gachman's blog *Bureaucracy for Breakfast* has been featured on NPR, AOL, and *Chelsea Handler* and she writes for *Huffington Post*, *Marie Claire* and *Hello Giggles*. She writes the graphic novel *Fling Girl LA* and writes comic books for Bluewater Comics.

Born in Arizona into an Air Force family, **Trina Gaynon** traveled widely in her first eighteen years. She now volunteers with an adult literacy program. Her poems appear in two anthologies, as well as numerous journals.

Kirsten Giles is a learning specialist and the owner of a small corporate training company. When she's not creating training solutions for automotive companies, she's writing poetry and plays.

After a long career in communications, **Ellen Girardeau (Kempler)** is writing poetry again. She's the mama bird in the empty nest, the turncoat in the corporate army, the emerging poet in mid-life. She's still writing for pay – but the "mind space" for creative work is the real payoff.

Arlene Granadosin has a background in urban planning and history, which, in more ways than one, influences her poetry, short stories and non-fiction articles. She has recently discovered her love for writing haikus, especially with her mentee, Tiffany.

Rory Green is a writer with a Masters degree in Psychotherapy. Originally from the UK, she now lives in LA, where she facilitates Write To Be You Reflective Writing Workshops. Her weekly blog is packed full of encouraging writing prompts: www.writetobeyou.com

Silvie Grossmann is a writer, photographer and filmmaker, based in Los Angeles. She recently obtained her MFA at USC, and has been writing, directing and designing for film and TV. You can see more of her work at www.getoutofthebox.net

Christina Guillén teaches K-12 at the Corona-Norco Unified School District and is soon headed to the University of Central Florida to pursue her MFA in fiction. She writes on bicultural subjects under her alter ego, super-heroine, Half-Moon Jefa.

Good Girls Don't is the debut literary effort of entertainment publicist **Patti Hawn**. Patti resides in Manhattan Beach, California with her husband and travels to India, Nepal and Thailand, where she works in humanitarian efforts.

Originally from Hungary, **Anna Henry** studied Cinema/Television at USC and has worked on television shows and movies. She also does academic editing and writes a non-fiction book review blog. Besides writing and mentoring, she loves raising her two little boys.

Alison M. Hills, PhD, is a playwright and essayist. Her plays were produced at Stanford and UCLA, where they won playwriting competitions. She wrote and performed a piece for an LA production of *Expressing Motherhood*. She co-produces ALAP's (Alliance of L.A. Playwrights) New Works Lab with local LA theaters.

For nearly 10 years, **Ashaki M. Jackson** has been a WriteGirl mentor and volunteer. You can read her poetry in publications by Eleven Eleven, The Splinter Generation, The Drunken Boat, and TORCH, among others. She is also a social psychologist.

Brande Jackson is a writer, educator, entrepreneur, organizer and artist. In addition to working with WriteGirl, she runs an after-school non-profit called Living Histories, is a part-time lecturer in American Studies at CSUF, and is the founder of a small company called Lokahi.

Peggy Johnson is proud to be an LA native. "I *am* LA—I love WORDS—to read and write—to cry, to laugh, to sigh right into an alternate state of relish—of writing poetry, novels—and wordplay puzzles and puns." Go, Dodgers!

Rachel Kaminer is a poet who grew up in the mountains of Asheville, North Carolina, and moved to Los Angeles in 2011 to pursue her MFA – and join WriteGirl! She loves playing outside and exploring the neighborhoods of her adopted city.

Devon Kelly is a film and television writer who is about to begin her third season as a writer/producer on the sitcom *Happily Divorced* on TVLand. Before that, she worked for a Disney website, writing sketch comedy.

Porter Kelly is an LA-based actor and writer. She wrote and performed at ACME Comedy Theatre for six years. Recent TV credits include *The Office, Private Practice, Lie to Me, Law & Order: LA*, and *New Girl*. www.porterkelly.com

Inspired by each new day, **Karen Knighton** has been writing in her journals since the age of eight. Today, she is an experienced writer and editor in the magazine and publishing fields, with a focus on creative writing.

Kendra Kozen is an award-winning journalist whose work appears in print and online. She holds a Masters degree from the University of Southern California and has been involved with WriteGirl since 2008. Recently married, Kendra enjoys working and living in LA.

Elline Lipkin is a poet, scholar, and nonfiction writer. Her first book, *The Errant Thread*, was selected by Eavan Boland for the Kore Press First Book Award. Her second book, *Girls' Studies*, was published by Seal Press in 2009.

Suzan Alparslan Lustig is a Pushcart-nominated poet whose work has been published in several journals. She holds an MFA in Creative Writing from Antioch University, and balances her literary endeavors with hands-on work as a massage therapist.

Brooklyn-born **Reparata Mazzola** is a published author, produced screenwriter and Emmy-nominated writer/producer. A member of Barry Manilow's back-up trio, Lady Flash, she recorded 7 albums, appeared on 2 TV specials and toured the world. Currently, she has 3 films in development.

Jessica McCarthy is an event planner, designer and coordinator who has worked on both corporate and private events from LA to Las Vegas. Her past nonprofit experience includes volunteering with Reading to Kids, Philanthropic Society of Los Angeles and Children's Institute, Inc. She comes to WriteGirl eager to fuse her professional experience with what she holds dear – ensuring that girls have role models to help navigate their path to becoming remarkable adults, and a love of literature, in particular.

Jessica McKay is a 5th grade English teacher at the Center for Early Education. She loves working with her students and WriteGirl mentees on writing memoirs and other creative nonfiction pieces.

Poet, journalist, screenwriter, blogger and author, **Monice Mitchell Simms** writes "because not breathing is not an option." She recently completed her first novel, *Address: House of Corrections*, and is currently penning a book of poetry and a follow-up novel, *The Mailman's Daughter*.

Chelsey Monroe is a novel writer and movie producer, having written three novels, and produced over 13 short films and segments. She currently works as the Production Coordinator for TakePart TV, and graduated from UCLA with a degree in Theater.

Jennifer Notas has written four Hallmark Channel movies: *Elevator Girl, Gift of the Magi, Keeping Up with the Randalls*, and *A Taste of Romance*, which was the number one movie of the week among its key demographic.

Niya Palmer mistakenly attempted a career in public relations. After billing clients for "a whole bunch of nothing" and several bad performance reviews, she decided to become a television writer. Most recently, she worked on Disney Channel's *Ant Farm*.

Carly Pandza is a loud and proud Croatian Scorpio, San Diego Native, Chapman University/ SAS alumni, arts enthusiast, filmmaker, writer and actress with insatiable wanderlust! Carly loves WriteGirl because it combines two of her passions – writing and empowering young women!

Blazhia Parker is a poetry, prose and nonfiction novice/writer. She likes to use her passion for writing and film to encourage other writers and readers to explore, enjoy, but also question and search for meaning through each experience with art.

Jackie Parker is the author of the novels *Our Lady of Infidelity* and *Love Letters to My Fans* (YA). Her play, Absentia, premieres in New York in the fall of 2012. She has received fellowships in fiction (The MacDowell Colony) and poetry.

Ingrid Carolina Parra just received a Masters Degree from Loyola Marymount University. She hopes to soon be admitted to a doctorate program, where she can one day become the leading specialist on the Amazon region. She hopes all women can find and utilize their voice.

Hunter Phillips is a writer, director, producer and principal at Free Radical Pictures. The young women of WriteGirl are a source of inspiration, levity and wit that Hunter continues to appreciate. She is honored to be a WriteGirl mentor.

Elda Pineda is the Program Manager for P.S. ARTS and is a proud advocate for arts education. In the fall, she will begin working on her Masters degree in Public Administration at USC, but hopes to write a few short stories in between research papers.

Retta Putignano King is the head writer at Create Your Reel, a company she co-owns. She has written over 3,000 scenes for actors' reels, and is currently working on a novel that fulfills her inner sappy romantic.

Marni Rader lives for WriteGirl events, the creative brilliance of her astoundingly talented mentee, Zoe Camp, indulging her book-buying addiction, concocting mini-cupcake delicacies, capitulating to her Chihuahuas, Tinker and Taco, and letting her keyboard rip for fun and profit.

India Radfar is the author of four books of poetry and a chapbook. Her new poetry manuscripts are nearing completion. She is also at work on a book about her in-laws, who still speak Aramaic to each other in their daily lives. She is the mother of Aram, 14 and Leila, 5.

Anne Ramallo has merged writing with an interest in design that originated when a college roommate introduced her to *Trading Spaces*. She is the author of *Outdoor Rooms II* and Manager of PR and Marketing at the product design firm Karten Design.

Sandra Ramos O'Briant is the author of *The Sandoval Sisters' Secret of Old Blood* (La Gente Press, summer 2012). Please visit her at www.thesanovalsisters.com for a complete list of her published work.

Diahann Reyes is a writer, actor, editor, and freelance journalist. She has worked for CNN, in public relations, and was www.FindLaw.com's first Executive Editor. Diahann writes memoir, nonfiction and poetry. She supports women and girls in their authentic, full self-expression.

Liz Rizzo has been a dreamer since 1971, an Angelino since 2002, and blogger since 2005. Pieces of her soul hover over West Palm Beach, the FSU Film School lobby, and above the stars on Hollywood Blvd. Her heart she brings with her, bruises and all.

Alicia Ruskin's career as a commercial talent agent has taught her about the power of language and image to persuade, and her time with WriteGirl has taught her that independent thought is a learned and necessary skill.

Vera Santamaria is a television writer whose credits include *Community and Outsourced*. A Toronto native, Vera began her career in Canada, making her way onto the country's biggest shows, including *Little Mosque on The Prairie* and *Degrassi: The Next Generation*.

Amy Silverberg is a writer living in Los Angeles. Her stories have appeared in the *Los Angeles Review*, Lumina, online at ThoughtCatalog, and elsewhere. She received her Masters in Fiction at the University of Southern California.

In the first or second grade, **Inez Singletary** noticed that all of the sample sentences the teacher gave the class began with "I." Her thought was, "Every sentence does not begin with 'I'." A writer was born. Inez feels that her mentee's development is bliss.

Valencia Walker is a Southern belle who moved to Los Angeles to work as a doctor. She loves writing, because it perfectly immortalizes emotions and feelings. She also enjoys mentoring young people and helping them find their own unique writing voices.

Kristen Waltman is currently working in the ever-evolving world of social media as a ghostwriter for various "celebrities" whom she is not allowed to name…sorry! She received her BA in Journalism from Michigan State University. This is her third year as a WriteGirl mentor.

Mentoring and teaching fashion and writing to youth has become a true love for **Jessica Williams**. She is an advocate for many youth programs geared towards promoting the arts and literacy. Her motto is: "You have to attempt to error to correct to succeed!"

Maiya Williams has been writing television for 25 years. Credits include *The Fresh Prince of Bel-Air, MAD TV* and *Futurama*. She also writes Young Adult novels, including *The Golden Hour Trilogy* and *The Fizzy Whiz Kid*.

Jacqueline Wilson hails from Brooklyn, New York. Currently, she works as a Supervising Producer on the successful reality franchise, *RuPaul's Drag Race*. She's a graduate of Syracuse University and the recipient of the prestigious Bill Cosby Screenwriting Fellowship.

Melissa Wong is a television writer living in Los Angeles. Her credits include *The 63rd Annual Emmy Awards, The MTV Movie Awards* and NBC's hit show, *The Voice*. This is her fifth year as a WriteGirl mentor.

Index

About the Publisher/Editor and WriteGirl Leadership

Keren Taylor, Founder and Executive Director of WriteGirl, has been active as a community leader for more than 18 years. She has edited and designed dozens of anthologies and has served as publisher and editor of all of WriteGirl's award-winning books. Passionate about helping women and girls, Keren has conducted hundreds of creative writing workshops for youth and adults, and has led staff development workshops for the California Paraeducators Conference, California School-Age Consortium, California Department of Education, Los Angeles County Office of Education, L.A.'s BEST and the New York Partnership for After School Education, among others. Keren has been selected to serve as a Community Champion and facilitator for the Annenberg Alchemy Program and is a popular speaker at conferences and book festivals nationwide, including the Association of Writing Programs Annual Conference, BOOST Conference, Los Angeles Times Festival of Books and Guiding Lights Festival. Keren is the recipient of numerous awards and accolades, including the President's Volunteer Call to Service Award, Business & Professional Women's Community Woman of Achievement Award, Soroptomist International's Woman of Distinction Award, commendations from Los Angeles Mayor Antonio Villaraigosa and others.

Keren is an assemblage artist and mosaicist. Her artwork has been exhibited at the The Annex L.A., Barnsdall Art Center, Gallery 727, Rock Rose Gallery and Shambhala Center Los Angeles, and is in personal collections. Her assemblage works are featured on the book covers of WriteGirl anthologies. She holds a Bachelor's Degree in International Relations from the University of British Columbia, a Piano Performance Degree from the Royal Conservatory of Music, Toronto, and a Diploma from the American Music and Dramatic Academy, New York City. Keren has overseen WriteGirl's expansion into a thriving community of women and teen writers and an organization that helps hundreds of Los Angeles girls annually.

Allison Deegan serves as WriteGirl's Associate Director and has provided critical strategic and operational guidance since the organization's inception in 2001. She participates in all aspects of WriteGirl's leadership, programming and sustainability, and also serves on the WriteGirl Advisory Board. Professionally, Allison is a Business Manager with the Los Angeles County Office of Education, following a career as a marketing and financial consultant. She has made numerous presentations around the country on topics related to after school program success, creative writing and working with youth. She is a mentor, trainer and curriculum consultant with the California School-Age Consortium, which provides professional development to after school program staff. She holds a B.S. in Marketing from Syracuse University, a Master's Degree in Public Policy from California State University, Long Beach, and a Doctorate in Educational Leadership, also from CSULB. Allison is a screenwriter and fiction writer and has remained close to her WriteGirl mentee, who is currently in graduate school.

About WriteGirl

WriteGirl, a creative writing organization for teens, was founded in 2001 in Los Angeles. Through mentoring relationships with professional women writers, workshops, readings and publications, WriteGirl's innovative program offers girls techniques and insights in all genres of writing, helping them to develop communication skills, confidence, self-esteem and an expanded view of themselves and their futures. WriteGirl was awarded a Medal for Service and named the 2010-2011 California Nonprofit of the Year by First Lady Maria Shriver and Governor Arnold Schwarzenegger. In September 2010, WriteGirl received the HUMANITAS Philanthropy Prize, acknowledging WriteGirl's outstanding work of encouraging and empowering writers. WriteGirl is a project of nonprofit organization Community Partners.

**WriteGirl welcomes your support and involvement:
visit WriteGirl on the web at www.writegirl.org**